SHIPWRECKS OF THE ATLANTIC

Montauk to Cape May

SHIPWRECKS OF THE ATLANTIC
Montauk to Cape May

Bill Davis

THE FISHERMAN LIBRARY
by Ocean Sport Fishing
1620 Beaver Dam Road
Point Pleasant, NJ 08742

Printed in the United States of America

Library of Congress Cataloging-in-Publication data

ISBN 0-923155-12-0

THE FISHERMAN LIBRARY
Ocean Sport Fishing
1620 Beaver Dam Road
Point Pleasant, NJ 08742

Copy Editing . . . . Linda Barrett
Production . . . . Matt Muzslay
Art Direction . . . . . . Steve and Terri Goione

ACKNOWLEDGMENTS

In appreciation for all their support, time and knowledge, I would like to thank the following divers, fishermen and friends for their assistance in making this book possible; my dive partners John McLinden, George Price and Joe Paola; fishing and diving expert Captain John Larsen of the Deep Adventures II from Point Pleasant, New Jersey; Captains Ed Eglentowicz and John Zlotnik from the dive boat Robin II, located in Barnegat, New Jersey; my fishing partners John "Poppy" Blum, Steve Waterson, Ryan Waterson and Jerry LeFevers; my wife Donna who understands why I have to fish or dive almost every weekend; and a very special thank you to fellow diver and good friend Joe Milligan for the vast amount of help he has given with his historical expertise and dive knowledge.

TABLE OF CONTENTS

INTRODUCTION

Thousands of ships have met their fate off the coast of New Jersey and New York at the hands of the unpredictable Atlantic Ocean. It is difficult to account for the actual number of shipping disasters that occurred prior to 1750 because of the lack of local news publications and the undeveloped population along the coastline. Historical data was often lost with the crew of the vessel when she broke up in the surf, or was taken to the graves of the old salts. The stories that survived often report conflicting facts since survivors, in their panic, remember the facts differently. After reading varying testimonies, the ones that appear the most rational will be discussed in this book.

Countless reasons can be given as to why so many ships have wrecked off the mid-Atlantic shore. In colonial times the lack of navigational aids caused many wrecks. Many vessels ran aground believing they had clear passage. Early navigational charts marked shoals of uncertain position and even on calm, clear days a captain might have found his vessel in danger. During the 17th century, much of the coastline was undeveloped so there were few lights that could be spotted along the shore making navigating on a dark night very hazardous.

Derelicts added to the list of hazards encountered by early mariners. Derelicts are partially submerged ships that were lost at sea and refused to sink to the ocean floor. Continuously being driven by the currents, they strike fear in the heart of every sea captain. The United States Hydrographic Office conducted a seven year study from 1887 to 1893, during which an average of 232 derelicts were sighted yearly, for a total of 1,628 over the seven years.

There have been many well-known derelicts throughout history. One was the four masted schooner William L. White. Abandoned off the Delaware Capes in a blizzard in 1888, the floating, half-submerged vessel was believed to have caused many shipwrecks while she remained afloat. Her final resting place was recorded off Scotland after she finally ran aground. Another derelict, the Fannie E. Woolston, was abandoned at sea October 15, 1891 off Virginia. She was positively identified forty-five times until her last sighting on October 21, 1894. It is believed that during those three years, the derelict covered over 10,000 miles of ocean.

This old sailing ship was one of the many ships that became victim to the New Jersey coast because their captains were unfamiliar with the eastern coast. Photo by Bill Schmoldt.

THE FIRST RECORDED SHIPWRECK:

Perhaps the earliest recorded shipwreck off the New Jersey/New York coast was a Dutch vessel that came ashore near modern day Sandy Hook in 1640. Among the ship's passengers was the Princess Penelope Van of Holland. She and her husband were on their way to New Amsterdam, known today as New York, when the ship was driven ashore in a severe storm. Many passengers aboard lost their lives in the sinking and most of those who survived sustained serious injuries.

Those capable of continuing on, formed a rescue party and salvaged enough timbers to make a small boat. They sailed north to New Amsterdam intending to return to rescue the others. Because Penelope's husband was severely injured in the incident and could not be moved, she stayed behind with her loved one awaiting the return of the rescue party.

Shortly after the sailing party departed, the remaining group came under attack by the local Indians. Penelope's husband was killed, as were many of the others, and Penelope herself was seriously injured. She hid in a hollow tree for seven days, feeding on the sap. She was traded by the Indians to the Dutch for valuables. Penelope later remarried and settled in Middletown, New Jersey where she lived to be 110 years old. This story survived primarily because Penelope Van lived to such an old age.

REVOLUTIONARY WAR WRECKS:

From 1650 until 1750 little is found in the history books about sea disasters along the eastern seaboard. The era of the Revolutionary War, however, brought many ships to the American coast. Sailing ships carrying cargo for the British soldiers and vessels heavily laden with arms to support the war effort patrolled the coast daily. Many of these ships wrecked because their captains were unfamiliar with the eastern coast. One report states that on December 9, 1778, fourteen British vessels wrecked in a heavy snowstorm off the Atlantic Highlands. Unfortunately for the modern historian or scuba diver, these ships have never been located.

Of the many vessels lost off the coast during the American Revolutionary War, few can be accounted for today. There are however, the remains of several American Colonial ships in the Mullica River. They were captured by the British during the war and destroyed in the confines of the river. These wrecks are under the protection of the state of New Jersey and cannot be disturbed.

Early Life Saving Stations were credited for saving thousands of lives because of the dedicated men and women who risked their lives to help save others. Photo by Bill Schmoldt.

THE LAND PIRATES:

Shortly after the Revolutionary War a group of blood-thirsty men and women who lived off the tragedy of the war began pirating along the shoreline. This group later came to be known as the "Land Pirates." During the evening, usually when clouds covered the moon and stars, the Land Pirates would walk a donkey along the ridge of a sand dune. Around the donkey's neck would hang a lantern, mimicking another ship or lighthouse. A captain would alter his course to move toward this light and would run aground. The Land Pirates would then attack the vessel killing all those aboard and stealing whatever they could carry.

When the seas were rough, ships would often break apart drowning those who could not swim, performing the dirty deed for the pirate. One legend tells of a young couple from Long Island who were soon to be married. They were temporarily separated when the young man sailed back to England to receive his dowry. Unbeknownst to him, his fiance and her father were Land Pirates.

While working one night on the beach, they spotted a vessel off the shore heading in their direction. High atop a sand dune the girl walked the donkey in a large circle. The wary ship's crew headed their ship toward what they believed was safe harbor beyond the lighthouse. The vessel struck the bar and overturned, throwing the entire crew into the water where they drowned. While scouring the beach for valuables, the young girl found her fiance dead on the beach. It was his ship returning from England with presents for his future bride. It is told that she died a widow with a broken heart. Whether this story is true or not, will never be known. It is true, however, that Land Pirates roamed the eastern shores and caused hundreds, if not thousands, of shipwrecks.

THE EARLY LIFE SAVING STATIONS:

Until the mid-nineteenth century, little could be done when a ship ran aground. Locals helped as much as possible, and if there were any survivors, a bit of history would endure. In 1848, the Life Saving Service was established. For the next thirty years the stations operated with limited guidance from the federal government and little in the way of rescue equipment. The men and women who served as Life Savers were dedicated and often risked their own lives to save another.

Mr. Joseph Francis of Toms River, New Jersey, worked four years to perfect a life saving device that would carry those held captive aboard a sinking vessel to safety. The lifeboat he designed resembled a pea pod, fully enclosed by a very small entrance that could be secured shut. A rope was shot out to the stricken vessel, the line was secured at both ends, and the lifeboat hauled out to sea. Once the stranded passengers were inside, the lifeboat was pulled back to shore. The device, named for its inventor, became known as the Francis Life Car and while used in rescue operations, saved thousands of lives. It was during this time period that written documentation of shipwrecks began to be compiled by the Life Saving Stations. In 1871, the Life Saving Service became officially recognized by the government and remained in existence until 1915 when it was renamed and merged with the United States Coast Guard.

THE GERMAN WOLFPACK:

In 1917, World War I came to the United States coast in the form of German submarines. The German Wolfpack, as it was called,

German submarines were credited for the destruction of hundreds of vessels during World War I and World War II. Photo by Joe Milligan.

roamed the Atlantic laying mines, shelling unarmed vessels and torpedoing any ships their paths might cross. One of the first war casualties off the American coast was the armed cruiser USS San Diego. She was sunk by a mine placed by a German submarine off Fire Island, New York. The history of the sinking of this vessel as well as others occuring during the war is covered in this book. During the United States' four year involvement, over 350 vessels were sunk. Only a handful of these have ever been located.

One that is still waiting to be found is the Subchaser No. 209. On August 27, 1918 she was lost south of Long Island, reported sunk by gunfire from a deck gun of a German submarine. A Naval investigation of the sinking reported, however, that the Subchaser had been mistaken as an enemy vessel and fired upon by the American Steamship Felix Taussig. Eighteen of her crew were killed in the incident and four others were wounded. To date, the remains of the Subchaser No. 209 have not been positively identified. It is possible she is being fished or dove by locals who know her only as a snag.

WORLD WAR II:

More than 20 years later, in 1942, the American shores were once again under attack. This time the German U-boat fleet was larger and more sophisticated. They attacked frequently and inflicted serious damage to the ships of the United States and her allies. Along the East Coast from New York to North Carolina, over 100 vessels were sunk resulting in countless casualties.

One of the first to fall victim was the Norwegian ship Norness. On January 4, 1942 she was enroute from New York to Halifax with a load of fuel oil. The unfortunate Norness was spotted by Commander Hardegen of U-boat 123, sixty miles off Montauk. In the early morning while most of the Norwegian crew were below decks asleep, a torpedo tore into the port side of the Norness. The men scrambled onto the decks to fight for their lives. As they attempted to lower the ship's lifeboats, two more torpedoes ripped into the stricken ship sending her to the bottom. Few survivors lived to tell of this horrifying experience.

Over the next three years many more casualties of World War II would be recorded off the East Coast. It wasn't until 1945, when America and her allies won the war that shipping was no longer in danger of an enemy it could not see.

MODERN DAY DISASTERS:

For the past forty-five years, there has been no war to blame for the destruction of men and their vessels at sea. The construction of modern ships with sophisticated, electronic equipment have enabled vessels to navigate the rough weather and foggy shorelines with greater safety. The latest, modern masterpiece, the computer, has also contributed to the decrease in disasters at sea, but there is still, and will always be, the human element which accounts for some of the modern day shipwrecks. One such mishap was the sinking of the forty-eight foot charter fishing boat, Joan La Rie III.

Although it was never publicly determined that she succumbed to human error, she did sink. According to one survivor's account, eight miles east of the Manasquan Inlet, the Joan La Rie III was gently picked up by a giant wave which laid the charter vessel on her side. The boat remained afloat for fifteen minutes or so, then sank to the bottom. Eight men, including the captain, lost their lives. A Coast Guard inquiry, which lasted nearly two years, found no definite cause of the sinking. One local diver who was the first to dive the wreck discovered that one of the bilge pumps had been

This sportfishing boat is just one of the many vessels that met their fatal destinies every year due to accidents on the high seas. Photo by Pete Barrett.

disconnected from the outlet post, causing water to circulate internally and remain in the boat's belly. This is a possible answer to the mystery, but will never be confirmed.

THE ARTIFICIAL REEF PROGRAM:

Recognizing the need to help mother nature and the many sea creatures that depend upon shipwrecks, the artificial reef has been developed. With the assistance of many public and governmental organizations, obstructions are placed on the ocean floor to serve as shelters and breeding grounds for the species that live beneath the surface.

There are many artificial reefs off the New York and New Jersey coasts. One of these, the "Sea Girt Reef," is made up of more than ten vessels. At an approximate depth of eighty feet are the remains of a dry dock (100'x50'), a railroad barge (200'x60'), the 70 foot clam boat Carlson II, the 205 foot ferry boat Cranford, the 85 foot tugboat Spartan and the 95 foot tugboat Rockland County. These artificial obstructions have proven to be beneficial to not only the sea life, but to fishermen and divers as well.

The Spartan is a main attraction for both divers and fishermen who work the Sea Girt Reef. Photo by Herb Segars.

The 165′ freighter Pauline Marie being towed into position on the Atlantic City Reef. Photo by Pete Barrett.

The Fisherman's Sport Fishing Fund and private donations enabled Bill Figley of New Jersey's Bureau of Marine Fisheries to put the Pauline Marie to her final resting place on the Atlantic City Reef. Photo by Pete Barrett.

FISHING AND DIVING ON WRECKS:

There are many attractions that lure people into diving and fishing on wrecks. Probably the single most important is the fascination with the unknown. All wreck divers can recall the thoughts, "What's down there? Are there any sharks lurking just beyond the horizon of visibility? How did this vessel sink? Did anyone die in the mishap? How did the survivors persevere? Did those who died suffer greatly?" These and many other questions run through a diver's or fisherman's mind while they are working on a wreck.

There are many levels of recreational diving from a basic certification to a "five-star" instructor. In the dive community there are many different styles with varying interests. The most common in New Jersey and New York are the "Bug (lobster) Divers." Ascending to wrecks or obstructions with an average depth of 80 feet, they swim in and around the debris field searching for this delicacy of the sea. Lobster vary substantially in size and weight, with the average bug weighing 2 to 3 pounds. Lobster are sometimes caught weighing as much as ten pounds, and quite infrequently, twenty pounds or more.

This successful catch of "Bugs" will make some very fine dining for a happy crew.

Another type of diver in this region is the "Artifact Hunter." Often geared up with hammer, chisel, wrenches, crow-bar and liftbag, these divers could be misconstrued as underwater car mechanics. In search of a remnant from the past, this diver spends his time usually digging in the same spot, never seeing but a few feet of the wreckage. A treasure to the artifact hunter could be anything from a brass valve to a pirates chest filled with gold doubloons.

Spearfishermen have become very common off mid-Atlantic coast. Many divers have taken up the sport and those who have made this their specialty have been rewarded with some excellent catches. Spearfishing can be dangerous, however. Those interested should seek the proper training and start with smaller species of fish before tackling game fish.

Underwater photography has recently become a large attraction. With the water clarity improving the environment for photography is no longer limited to the tropics. Many days the visibility off the Eastern coast exceeds fifty feet making the beauty of the local wrecks an excellent backdrop for photographs.

For these happy "Artifact Hunters" a collection of Prohibition liquor bottles were a lucky find. Photo by Rick Schwarz.

Offshore wrecks were a favorite spot for tuna fishermen looking for yellowfin and bluefin. Photo by Pete Barrett.

There is also the diver who just enjoys sightseeing. They thrive on the experience and sensation of being underwater, surrounded by beauty. It is likely that the sightseer appreciates diving the most. Although there are many other styles of diving, these are the most common in this region. One thing is certain, all divers depend greatly on shipwrecks for their treasures, their scenery and the sea life they attract.

Fishermen have been fascinated by wrecks, and the good fishing opportunities they present, for decades. The chance to catch large bottom dwellers like cod and pollock, bragging-sized blackfish and seabass, and pelagic species like sharks and tuna keep wrecks on the minds of many recreational fishermen.

While many fishermen believe wreck fishing is difficult because it may be hard to find the wreck itself, or that special gear is required to anchor near the wreck; the reality is that fishing a wreck is simple, productive and fun. You just have to try once and you will probably be hooked.

Other readers of this book may not be fishermen or divers, but history buffs who enjoy learning more about the rich past of the sea coast. The many stories and background of local shipwrecks makes terrific reading.

The Grumman Avenger TBM was the U.S. Navy's prime torpedo bomber during World War II.

AC AIRPLANE

VESSEL TYPE: AIRPLANE
DEPTH: 80 FEET
CONSTRUCTION: STEEL
LOCATION: 26855.5/43113.5

Approximately ten miles east of the Beach Haven Inlet are the remains of a World War II, Grumman Avenger aircraft. The wreckage is not as massive as many of the shipwrecks off the coast, therefore few charter boats have been attracted to the site. She is visited by divers and a few local fishermen who have done very well on this unusual wreck. One such diver, Donald Southwick, has dove the wreck many times and has recovered two 50 caliber machine guns that were mounted on the Avenger's wings.

The airplane is fully intact resting upside down, half buried on the sandy ocean floor. Her profile is relatively low thus she may be difficult to find. Visibility often exceeds twenty feet and the wreck is an interesting subject for photographers. She is covered by a marine growth of coral and sea anemones.

Fisherman, Gordon Roberts, who owns and operates the Moose, sailing out of Tuckerton, often fishes the Avenger. Gordon noted that the wreck seems to attract ling, fluke and weakfish.

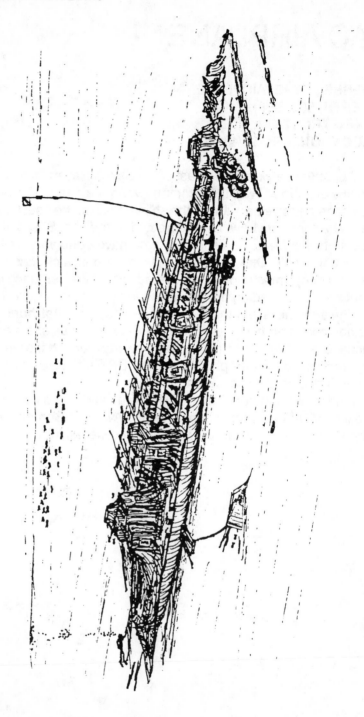

Adonis, underwater drawing by Al Hoffman.

ADONIS WRECK

BUILT: 1853
VESSEL TYPE: WOODEN BARK
LENGTH: UNKNOWN

LOST: MARCH 7, 1859
DEPTH: 20 FEET
LOCATION: 26950.2/43598.8

There is little known about the Dutch bark Adonis because of the time period in which she ran aground and sank. Built in 1853 and registered at 550 gross tons, she was valued at $20,000 and was owned by the F. Beck Company. Enroute from Newcastle, England to New York she encountered a southwest gale and ran aground off Long Branch, New Jersey. After all crew members and passengers were rescued, numerous attempts were made to free the vessel from the sand bar. On the morning of March 12th the ship finally gave in to the pounding sea and split in two.

An auction was held on the beach later that day and the vessel and her cargo were sold for $25.00. Anything else that could be salvaged from the sea would belong to her new owner. The cargo was said to have included grindstones, 170 casks of powder, 630 kegs of soda, 200 casks of red wine and 330 packages of miscellaneous merchandise. Much of this has not yet been recovered.

The Adonis lies almost completely covered by sand but is easily recognized by her wooden structure and decking which still protrude above the sand. Surprisingly enough, the wreck continues to yield artifacts. She sank with 600 pigs of lead stamped with the Dutch emblem, each weighing 112 pounds, which are still being recovered today. There is also plenty of ballast stone around the wreck site. From a fishing standpoint the Adonis is not noted to be a real fish producer.

A.G. Ropes aground off Island Beach State Park.

BARGES A.G. ROPES AND UNDAUNTED

BUILT: 1886
VESSEL TYPE: SCHOONER
  BARGE
LENGTH: 238 FEET

LOST: DECEMBER 25, 1913
DEPTH: 510 FEET
LOCATION: ISLAND BEACH
  STATE PARK

A Christmas gale greeted the small tug Edgar F. Luckenbach with a friendly welcome. The tug was towing two schooner barges, the 238 foot A.G. Ropes and the 307 foot Undaunted. Both barges were laden with coal consigned to the Hartford Railroad, to be delivered to Providence, Rhode Island.

Unsuccessfully riding the storm and in danger of sinking, the skipper of the Edgar F. Luckenbach decided to cut free his tow. He signaled Captain Olson of the A.G. Ropes and Captain Fickett of the Undaunted to inform them that they should lower their anchors and fend for themselves.

Before the tug could return for the stranded barges, both vessels were washed into the breakers and broke apart. All ten men aboard were believed to have drowned. The Edgar F. Luckenbach which was later sold and renamed the Cherokee, ironically, sank outside the Delaware Bay.

Today the Undaunted lies beyond the surf off Island Beach State Park. The A.G. Ropes lies scattered in the surf, north of the Undaunted. Part of her remains are buried on the beach, occasionally uncovered by a fierce storm. Many artifacts have been recovered from the site.

Akron, courtesy of the U.S. Coast Guard.

AKRON

BUILT: 1931
VESSEL TYPE: RIGID DIRIGIBLE
LENGTH: 785 FEET
LOST: APRIL 4, 1933

DEPTH: 105 FEET
LOCATION:
MAIN 26726.7/43076.0
TAIL: 26724.9/43076.7

The Akron, an airship and not a sea going vessel, was one of the many dirigibles purchased by the U.S. Navy during World War I. They patrolled the coast in search of enemy craft, especially submarines which could surface anywhere. Their other function was to assist the Coast Guard in search of vessels in distress.

The Akron left its hangar at the Naval Air Engineering Center in Lakehurst, New Jersey at 7:30 p.m. on April 3rd. She was enroute to New England on a practice mission. She lifted off in the rain with poor visibility. As she made her way off the New Jersey coast a violent thunderstorm and heavy winds caught her. The winds overwhelmed the airship and caused the helium gas chambers to burst. She fell into the ocean, stern first, killing 73 of her 76 passengers and crew.

Until July 31, 1986, over fifty years after her demise, the whereabouts of the Akron were a mystery. Author Clive Cussler and his team of archeologists from the National Underwater and Marine Agency (NUMA) finally located the wreck. The wreckage was scattered in pieces ranging from 30 to 120 feet in length. The tail section was located several yards away from the main body of the dirigible.

Today the Akron lies in 105 feet of water some forty miles off the coast. Few have dove the wreck due to the distance from shore and the unknown of what an airship is like underwater. From a fishing standpoint the area produces well with all species of bottom dwellers.

Young seabass keep close to their hiding places within decaying hulls of wrecks. Photo by Herb Segars.

ALEX GIBSON

BUILT: EARLY 1900s   **LOST:** 1930s
VESSEL TYPE: WOODEN BARGE   **DEPTH:** 28 FEET
LENGTH: APPROX. 180 FEET   **LOCATION:** 27027.3/42750.0

Resting in 28 feet of water, ten miles off Cape May, are the remains of the Alex Gibson. Very little can be found in the history journals about the Gibson, primarily because there were no lives lost and no act of great heroism. The vessel is only remembered by those who have fished or dived her remains.

Today the remains of the Alex Gibson make excellent refuge for all types of sea creatures. The wreck lies low to the sand and has many hiding places within her decaying hull. The wreck is mostly intact with a length of approximately 180 feet. In the summer months she is home to seabass, which number in the thousands. Visibility is generally good because the remains lie on the sandy bottom. Also due to her shallow depth the wreck gets plenty of sunlight. For both novice divers and fishermen this is an excellent South Jersey site.

Almirante, photo by Joe Milligan.

ALMIRANTE

BUILT: 1909
VESSEL TYPE: PASSENGER
   FREIGHTER
LENGTH: 378 FEET

LOST: SEPTEMBER 6, 1918
DEPTH: 70 FEET
LOCATION: 26918.0/43025.7

The United Fruit Company steamship left the pier of New York City bound for the West Indies with a general cargo. Because of the ongoing submarine attacks off the Jersey coast, the seven passengers and ninety-eight crew members were extensively drilled in emergency procedures. This practice no doubt attributed to many lives being saved during the next 24 hours.

At 2:00 a.m. in rough seas, the Almirante crew watched helplessly when out of the fog, the bow of the Navy vessel USS Hisko rammed them. The Almirante sank in less than five minutes. Many of the crew members jumped overboard and were later rescued. Of the one hundred and five aboard, only five lost their lives in the incident.

To assure safe navigation the Almirante was blown up and wire dragged many times to reduce the ship to steel rubble. The wreck lies scattered on the ocean floor in 70 feet of water. This is a great site for student divers because it is shallow and offers lobster, artifacts and plenty of scenery. Sandy patches harbor fluke who in turn prey on the baitfish seeking shelter within the wreckage. Seabass, blackfish, eel pouts and ling are frequently spotted by divers.

Andrea Doria listing to starboard after the collision with the Stockholm.

ANDREA DORIA

BUILT: 1950
VESSEL TYPE: LUXURY LINER
LENGTH: 700 FEET

LOST: JULY 25, 1956
DEPTH: 225 FEET
LOCATION: 25147.7/43480.8

At 11:22 p.m. on July 25, 1956 the Andrea Doria was sailing toward port on the final evening of an uneventful four thousand mile voyage from Genoa, Italy. She was just fifty miles south of Nantucket Island when the Swedish vessel, Stockholm, appeared out of the fog. She collided with the Andrea Doria cutting an 80 foot hole in her forward section causing the liner to quickly fill with water and list badly to her starboard side. Fortunately for most of the 1,241 passengers and 575 crew members, the Doria stayed floating for over eleven hours. Forty-six lives were lost in the collision.

Today the wreckage of the Andrea Doria attracts experienced, trained deep divers and fishermen. One of those is Gary Gentile from Philadelphia, Pennsylvania who has made over seventy dives on the wreck. Gary knows the Doria better than most and has written many articles and a book, "Dive To An Era," about the history and his experiences during those dives.

Today the wreck lies on her port side, 225 feet beneath the surface. She is fully intact but shows signs of heavy deterioration. Large nets from draggers cover parts of the wreckage. From a fishing perspective, cod and pollack are caught on the wreck year-round. Sharks have made the wreck normal cruising grounds searching for an easy meal. Many anglers troll the area in the early fall for tuna which migrate over the Andrea Doria.

Antioch aground off the beach at Manasquan.

ANTIOCH

BUILT: 1876
VESSEL TYPE: TWO MASTED
  SCHOONER
LENGTH: 180 FEET

LOST: MARCH 27, 1913
DEPTH: 15 TO 20 FEET
LOCATION: NORTH END
  OF MANASQUAN

During a southeast gale the barkentine Antioch was washed ashore off Manasquan Beach, New Jersey. The 986 ton vessel, was carrying a cargo of railroad timbers bound for New York. Captain Morris, commander of the Antioch, immediately sent up a distress signal that caught the attention of the Life Saving Station Keeper, Longstreet of Squan Beach. The captain of the Life Saving Station called for his men as well as the assistance of the Spring Lake Life Saving crew.

After twelve hours of hard labor, all ten crew members of the Antoich were safely brought ashore. Unfortunately the vessel herself was not so lucky. Continuously being pounded by the growing waves, she broke apart and sank.

According to Bill Schmoldt, owner of the Brielle Dive Center and Maritime Bookstore, the wreck is located at the northern end of the Manasquan boardwalk. To reach the vessel from the beach you line up the pointed rock at the end of the jetty with the standpipe behind the beach badge house. The wreckage rests with the bow facing the east in 15 to 20 feet of water, approximately 150 feet off the end of the jetty.

Bill noted that the main body of the vessel is still intact with many smaller pieces scattered in the sand surrounding it. The anchor and chain lie on the sand just off the bow. There are a variety of bottom fish located on and about the wreck. The most noted are large blackfish that weigh five to seven pounds.

S.S. Arundo, courtesy of the U.S. Coast Guard.

S.S. ARUNDO

BUILT: 1930   **LOST:** APRIL 28, 1942
VESSEL TYPE: FREIGHTER   **DEPTH:** 130 FEET
LENGTH: 412 FEET   **LOCATION:** 26792.4/43515.1

The Arundo left the docks of New York at 5:00 a.m. on April 28th with a crew of 43 aboard. The 5,079 ton, steel hull Dutch freighter was built in 1930 by the Northlumberland Shipbuilding Corporation of New Castle, England. She was bound for the Allied Middle East Command in Capetown, South Africa with military supplies. These included vehicle parts, 123 trucks, two steam locomotives and coal tenders.

At 9:30 a.m. the Arundo was heading towards the Ambrose Light Station when the officer on watch sighted an object approaching off the starboard beam. As it neared the ship it was recognized as a torpedo, however, it was too late for the steamer to avoid the water borne missile.

The lethal torpedo hit fatally, directly under the Arundo's bridge. Water poured into the holds, flooding them instantly and causing the ship to sink toward the bow. The crew boarded lifeboats and abandoned the ship. As the Arundo sank, one of the locomotives toppled off the deck and fell on four crewmen, killing them instantly.

The sinking of the Arundo, was not made public at the time, since most of the German U-boat activity in America was considered classified by the military and government. It was not until after the war that fishermen and divers found her.

The Arundo lies in 125 feet of water, 22 miles northeast of Manasquan Inlet. The remains of the decaying vessel cover 400 feet of the ocean bottom and now serve as a bountiful, artificial reef. A few feet from the ship lies one of the locomotives, resting on its side. The second locomotive lies buried under debris, next to the outside bulkhead of the aftermost hold. Many interesting artifacts can be found on the Arundo with the most valuable ones, other than nautical, being measuring instruments which made up a small part of the cargo. For the fishermen, a day fishing on the wreck can be very rewarding. Not only do her remains supply shelter for bottom dwellers, she also attracts migrating bluefish and tuna during the late summer. Many shark fishermen consider the wreck a good area over which to drift or anchor. She's a favorite spot for giant tuna fishermen.

Astra, courtesy of The Steamship Historical Society, University of Baltimore Library.

ASTRA

BUILT: 1945
VESSEL TYPE: FREIGHTER
LENGTH: 333 FEET

LOST: MARCH 30, 1951
DEPTH: 85 FEET
LOCATION: 26901.2/43014.5

According to the Coast Guard report of April 26, 1951, the Astra departed Pier 14 in the East River, New York on March 30th bound for Havana, Cuba. She was carrying a cargo that consisted of automobiles, wool, lumber and general cargo.

On the same day, the much larger vessel, Steel Inventor, was traveling north towards New York to off-load her cargo. Because of the thick fog that had blanketed the area that morning, both captains gave the order to reduce speed and sound the fog horn at regulation intervals, fearing other vessels in the area. At approximately 6:00 a.m. Captain Axel Jelstrup, commander of the Astra, heard the horn of another vessel but could not distinguish in which direction it was moving. When the Steel Inventor came into sight, she was approximately three ship lengths away, approaching at an angle. Immediately Captain Jelstrup ordered full speed ahead and hard right rudder, thereby attempting to maneuver his vessel parallel to the Steel Inventor. In this way he hoped to minimize the damage sustained by his vessel since a collision was unavoidable. Unfortunately the vessels came together at such an impact that a gaping hole was torn in the port side of the Astra. She sank quickly by the stern leaving only her bow above water. The Steel Inventor's damage was minimal and her captain immediately had the anchor dropped. Lifeboats were launched to search for survivors of the Astra. Despite rough seas, heavy winds and poor visibility all the crew members from the ill-fated vessel were pulled to safety.

The remains of the Astra lie in 85 feet of water, 8.5 miles off the Absecon Inlet bell buoy. The stern and bow sections are mostly intact and rise 25 feet off the sea floor. Both sections can be easily penetrated by divers. The midsection is scattered over a large area and creates good homes for large lobster. Fishing the wreck will yield bottom dwellers, like seabass and blackfish. An occasional tropical fish may be found during the warmer summer months.

Atlanthus aground off Cape May.

ATLANTHUS

BUILT: 1918
VESSEL TYPE: CONCRETE
  FREIGHTER
LENGTH: 260 FEET

LOST: JUNE 8, 1926
DEPTH: 25 FEET
LOCATION: SUNSET BEACH,
  CAPE MAY

During World War I, the United States government declared a shortage of steel and began to search for alternative materials for ship construction. As an experiment thirty-eight vessels were commissioned to be built of concrete, of which only twelve were ever completed and put into service.

The Atlanthus, a 3,000 gross ton freighter, was built of a special aggregated concrete, five inches thick. She was completed November 21, 1918 by the Liberty Shipbuilding Corporation of Brunswick, Georgia. It would appear the concrete ship design was a failure for the Atlanthus since it was only in service for one year. The concrete ship proved unable to withstand heavy seas and she was removed from service. The end of the war was also the end of the Atlanthus. In 1920 she was purchased by a salvage company and scuttled of all her valuables.

In 1926 she was purchased by a Baltimore, Maryland firm that was planning to start a ferry service from Cape May, New Jersey to Lewes, Delaware. It was planned that the Atlanthus and two other vessels would be strategically positioned and sank, as they were to act as a landing for the ferry boats. On June 8th while awaiting her final resting place, a storm struck the Cape. She broke free of her mooring and came aground off the Shore of Sunset Beach, Cape May. Many attempts were made to free her, but she only sank deeper into the sand.

Today, the deteriorating remains of the concrete ship lie in 20 feet of water. The Atlanthus now serves as a shelter for the many small marine fish that inhabit her. The diver who wants to make the 200 foot swim off the beach should be cautioned that the deteriorating of the concrete has exposed the reinforcing rods used in the construction. The rusted, jagged steel can cause serious injury. This is a popular dive spot, especially for novices. The best time to dive the Atlanthus is when the seas are calm.

Ayuruoca, courtesy of the U.S. Coast Guard.

AYURUOCA

BUILT: 1912
VESSEL TYPE: FREIGHTER
LENGTH: 468 FEET

LOST: JUNE 10, 1945
DEPTH: 170 FEET
LOCATION: 26814.8/43547.2

The Ayuruoca left New York enroute to Brazil in a dense evening fog. On board were sixty-seven crewmen anticipating an uneventful journey south. She was a vessel of 6,872 gross tons, with a length of 468 feet, a 58 foot beam and a depth of 29 feet. Transporting a general cargo, she was filled with trucks, tools, cement, tea and metal products.

Fifteen miles south of Ambrose Light the Ayuruoca collided with the 5,138 ton Norwegian vessel General Fleischer. Fatally wounded, she only stayed afloat for a half hour. Fortunately for her crew, calm seas allowed them to lower the sinking ship's lifeboats with ease. Just one sailor lost his life in the incident.

The General Fleischer, in ballast and riding high above the water, only sustained a hole above the water line and was in no danger of sinking. Therefore she continued on to New York Harbor under her own power.

Today, the wreck of the Ayuruoca, often referred to as the "Oil Wreck," lies in 170 feet of water in the Mud Hole. She is split in half but the sections remain close together and the vessel appears to be fully intact. Due to her massive size and deep depth, it is not possible to see the entire wreck on one dive. Because the Ayuruoca is located in the Mud Hole, visibility is often limited to less than ten feet. Nevertheless the wreck site is impressive. She is sitting almost upright and rises sixty feet off the ocean floor.

On one particular charter, divers experienced a school of striped bass circling the wreck. Many of these fish were in the twenty pound range with a few being over fifty. On another occasion her remains appeared to be a hotel for ling. At every hole there were two or more occupying the space. The marine life on the Ayuruoca is in abundance with shell fish, bottom dwellers, migrating fish and mollusk. She is also a favorite for shark and giant tuna hunters.

AZUA

BUILT: 1918
VESSEL TYPE: FOUR MASTED
  SCHOONER
LENGTH: 171 FEET

LOST: MAY 14, 1930
DEPTH: 132 FEET
LOCATION: 26857.2/42804.9

On May 12, 1930 a dense fog covered the New Jersey coast line. For the experienced captain and owner of the 664 gross ton Azua, this was just another day. Captain J.A. McLean steered his vessel laden with coal out of New York harbor heading south for Bermuda.

Two days later, the steamship, City of Atlanta, left New York bound for Savannah, Georgia with passengers on board. Shortly after midnight, the much quicker City of Atlanta caught up to the freighter Azua and the two vessels collided in the fog. The passenger vessel sustained only minimal damage above the water line, but the freighter suffered a fatal blow and began to sink immediately. Captain Diehl of the City of Atlanta put out lifeboats to assist in the rescue of survivors. Eight of the eleven crew members survived. Among those lost, however, was Captain J.A. McLean and his first mate.

Because the Azua was considered a navigational hazard, the Coast Guard cutter Seneca was called upon to demolish the wreck to assure that there was a minimum of 60 feet of water over her grave.

Today the wreck of the Azua lies twenty-five miles off Great Egg Inlet in 120 feet of water. Some refer to this wreck as the "Huntington Barge." Others know her only as a snag. The few who have dove her remains noted the abundance of marine life on the wreck. They also commented that it appears few have fished the Azua because there is little monofilament on the wreck.

DORTHY B. BARRETT

BUILT: 1904
VESSEL TYPE: FIVE MASTED
  SCHOONER
LENGTH: 259 FEET

LOST: AUGUST 14, 1918
DEPTH: 60 FEET
LOCATION: 26963.4/42773.1

The story behind the sinking of the Dorthy B. Barrett makes an interesting story of a game of cat and mouse. The five masted schooner, carrying a cargo of coal was 259 feet in length, had a 45 foot beam with a draft of 25 feet. She was built and owned by the G.G. Deering Company from Bath, Maine and registered at 2,088 gross tons.

The ugly game began approximately twelve miles east of Cape May, New Jersey. The Dorthy B. Barrett was under full sail when the German submarine U-117, fired a shot across her bow, signalling her to stop. Fearing for their lives Captain William Merritt, skipper of the Barrett, ordered the lifeboat lowered and the passengers and crew to abandon ship. This was done quickly and the motorized lifeboat was soon a safe distance from the schooner.

Dorthy B. Barrett at port taking on cargo.

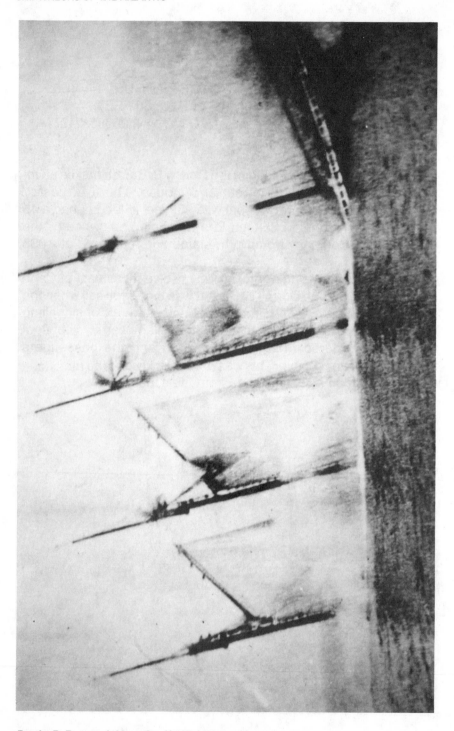

Dorthy B. Barrett sinking after U-117 destroyed her.

Out of curiosity, or perhaps seeking information about the doomed vessel, the commander of the U-117 pursued the motor boat. After they traveled some distance from the abandoned schooner, the U-boat turned back and destroyed the schooner. Meanwhile, the survivors aboard the motor boat were picked up by the U.S. Navy mine sweeper Kingfisher. At about the same time, the tanker William Green cruised into the vicinity of the disturbance.

After the Barrett sank below the surface, the U-117 headed toward shore, chasing both the Kingfisher and the William Green. The skippers of these two vessels, in an effort to save their ships, gave the order to run for shallow water. By doing this it was believed that the U-boat would have to give up the chase. A call for help was also dispatched by the two ships, now desperate for assistance.

The Navy dispatched four subchasers to their rescue, the submarine N-7 and also a seaplane. They all converged on the reported location. The U-boat was soon under attack by depth charges, aerial bombs and machine gun fire. It turned south and ran for deeper water. The small fleet and the seaplane chased the U-117 until she dove and could no longer be tracked. Unfortunately the U-117 escaped sinking, but the Dorthy B. Barrett didn't.

Joe Milligan, who has dove the Barrett many times, describes the wreck as a good lobster dive. The remains consist of three main pieces all low to the sand, rising only five feet off the bottom. The hull and decking are most recognizable and often parts or all of the wreck are covered over by sand. Lobster is the main attraction to the wreck, but some artifacts have been recovered. Bottom fish inhabit the wreckage and are plentiful. Joe commented that there isn't much monofilament on the wreck which indicates that it is not fished very hard.

S.S. Bidevind, courtesy of The Steamship Historical Society, University of Baltimore Library.

S.S. BIDEVIND

BUILT: 1938
VESSEL TYPE: FREIGHTER
LENGTH: 414 FEET

LOST: APRIL 30, 1942
DEPTH: 190 FEET
LOCATION: 26357.6/43280.4

Information concerning the history of this vessel, as with most World War II shipping disasters, is difficult to obtain. The Bidevind, a 414 foot Norwegian freighter, was built in 1938 by the Flensburg Shipbuilding Company. She weighed 4,956 gross tons and her cargo consisted of spices, oils and cashew nuts.

Part of a convoy heading to New York, the Bidevind met her fate when torpedoed 50 miles offshore of Manasquan Inlet by an unknown, and unseen German U-Boat.

Today, the intact wreck remains lie in 190 feet of water in the Mud Hole. The bow sits down, as if when she sank to the bottom, her nose plowed into the mud and remained that way. The dive is deep and dark, it should only be dove by experienced divers. The wreckage is home to cod and large numbers of pollock. Large blackfish are caught here along with ling and whiting and occasionally seabass.

Black Warrior

BLACK WARRIOR

BUILT: 1852
VESSEL TYPE: THREE MASTED
   PADDLEBOAT
LENGTH: 225 FEET

LOST: FEBRUARY 20, 1859
DEPTH: 30 TO 35 FEET
LOCATION: 26951.8/43755.3

The three masted Black Warrior was built in 1852 by William Collyer of New York. She was a steamship propelled with side paddle wheels and auxiliary sails. She was rated at 1,556 gross tons.

On two separate occasions prior to her sinking the Black Warrior made the news journals. In 1854 the Cuban government seized her in Havana during a mail delivery, which nearly lead to the United States declaring war with Cuba. The situation was resolved when the paddle boat was quickly released.

On the second occasion in 1857, the Black Warrior encountered a winter storm off Cape Hatteras, North Carolina. After combatting the storm for relentless hours she ran out of coal and was reduced to burning furniture and anything else that would burn. In this way she managed to limp back to port for refueling.

In 1859 the Black Warrior's luck finally ran out. Near the end of a journey on February 20th she entered New York Harbor in a heavy fog and ran aground off Long Island on Rockaway Bar.

After removing all the passengers and cargo, numerous attempts were made to free her. For four days everything, including coal and machinery was removed to lighten the load to float the Black Warrior free. Unfortunately before this was possible, a gale struck and smashed the vessel to pieces.

The Black Warrior lies in 30 to 35 feet of water, two miles east of the entrance to Rockaway Inlet. The wreckage is scattered over a large area but the paddle wheel is easily recognizable. Although not known as a fishing "hot spot" decent size fluke appear to be abundant, lying in and around the wreck. Seabass, ling and blackfish are also found among the scattered remains.

BRIAN C

BUILT: 1928
VESSEL TYPE: TUG BOAT
LENGTH: 80 FEET

LOST: NOVEMBER 13, 1979
DEPTH: UNKNOWN
LOCATION: 43 MILES EAST
ATLANTIC CITY

The exact location of the Brian C has yet to be discovered. It is quite possible that fishermen and divers visit her remains and are unaware of her identity or how she ended up on the bottom of the ocean.

Purchased by the Triangle Marine Corporation of Miami, Florida, her new owners planned to relocate the tug boat in Puerto Rico. They hired Captain J. Kirk Frazier of Coconut Grove, Florida and his team of three crew members to deliver the 136 gross ton boat to its new home port.

According to the Coast Guard inquiry, the following events preceded to the demise of the Brian C. In November, Captain Frazier arrived dockside at the Boston Fuel Transportation Company to take command of his vessel. A sea trial was performed at that time and minor repairs were made. After a second inspection, Captain Frazier felt the Brian C was ready for the voyage. Crew and stores were loaded, and on November 9th they set sail.

Approximately sixty miles southeast of Cape Cod Canal it was noticed that the stern was riding low in the water. Captain Frazier decided to return to port and have the vessel examined. It was discovered that three of the aft hatches had come open and the after ballast had filled with water. The tanks were pumped dry and examined for leaks. Upon completion of this and other inspections the hatches were welded closed. On November 12th once again the Brian C was off to sea.

The journey was uneventful until November 13th, when seventy miles off the New Jersey coast, Captain Frazier noticed his vessel was heavy in the stern. He attempted to radio the Coast Guard, but his radio wasn't reaching shore. Heading west towards Atlantic City, a mayday signal was sent but again there was no response. Finally forty-two miles offshore the mayday signal from the Brian C was received by the Coast Guard.

A helicopter was immediately dispatched. When the Coast Guard arrived on site, three of the tug's crew were removed and two Coast Guard crew members went aboard in an effort to save the ship. Pumps were then lowered on board as they attempted to remove the sea water. This attempt was abandoned since the water was coming in faster than it was being removed, and the Brian C was listing heavily to the port. Shortly afterwards the tug went under. The men were forced into the water where they were air lifted by the Coast Guard helicopter. To date the wreck of the Brian C has not been located.

BRUNETTE

BUILT: 1867
VESSEL TYPE: FREIGHTER
LENGTH: UNKNOWN

LOST: JANUARY 1, 1870
DEPTH: 75 FEET
LOCATION: 26916.4/43476.0

The steamfreighter Brunette was carrying a light load when she left the Lorillard Steamship dock bound for Philadelphia. Manned and operated by thirteen Philadelphian crewmen, the steamship was built in Wilmington, Delaware in 1867. She was owned by Jacob Lorillard, Jr., and was used primarily for coastal shipping between New York and Philadelphia. The vessel was a single screw propeller and weighed 274 gross tons.

On February 1st, at 10 o'clock on the evening, the watch on board spotted an unidentified ship headed toward them. Captain Doane of the Brunette, trying to avoid a collision, attempted to cut in front of the oncoming vessel. Before this could be achieved, she collided with the other ship, the Santiago de Cuba. The Brunette, struck broadside, began listing badly to the starboard. The crew took to the lifeboats and were assisted by the crew aboard the Santiago de Cuba. The severely damaged freighter was sent to the bottom in less than ten minutes, taking two crewmen with her.

Today, the wreck rests in 75 feet of water, three and a half miles off of Manasquan Inlet. The scattered wreckage is good for exploration and many fish and lobster can be found. Since the wreck was discovered, many artifacts have been recovered including such items as bottles, brass valves, pewter flatware, yardsticks, Missisaquoi spring water bottles, locks and door knobs, from which the wreck obtained the name "Door Knob Wreck."

CADET

BUILT: UNKNOWN
VESSEL TYPE: THREE MASTED
  SCHOONER
LENGTH: UNKNOWN

LOST: UNKNOWN
DEPTH: 80 FEET
LOCATION: 26916.4/43475.8

There is little historical information available about the wreck of the Cadet; only that she was a three masted vessel and sank approximately two miles off Bay Head, New Jersey in the late 19th century.

Today, the wreck of the Cadet is well known to local divers and on any given weekend you will be sure to find a boat anchored over her remains. The wreckage barely resembles the great sailing ship she once was. Her main beam is all that is recognizable and stretches some 200 feet north to south on the ocean floor. The wooden structure of the Cadet creates the perfect home for some of the largest lobster on the East Coast. An abundance of artifacts have also been taken including bottles, keys, brass and the ship's sextant. The fisherman will find that seabass and blackfish often school over the wreck. Normally the fish are smaller in size but they are abundant.

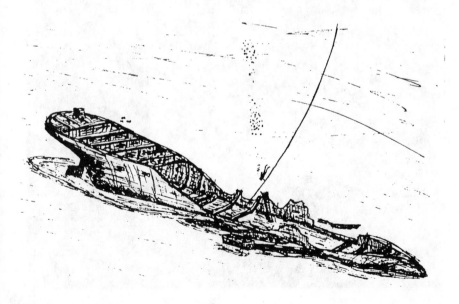

Cadet, underwater drawing by Al Hoffman.

Carolina in dry dock.

CAROLINA

BUILT: 1896
VESSEL TYPE: PASSENGER
  FREIGHTER
LENGTH: 380 FEET

LOST: JUNE 2, 1918
DEPTH: 250 FEET
LOCATION: APPROX.
  26453.0/42786.0

The Carolina was bound for New York from San Juan, Puerto Rico. On board, she was carrying 220 passengers and a crew of nearly one hundred. The 5,917 gross ton passenger freighter was making good time and her Captain anticipated an early arrival into New York Harbor.

It was to be the last evening on board and most of the passengers were enjoying dinner as they looked forward to the morning and their arrival at New York. Unfortunately they had expected to stroll off the decks of the Carolina, not swim off them!

Without warning, three shots were fired across the bow of the Carolina indicating to her Captain to shut down the engines. A boarding party from the German submarine that had been pursuing the Carolina rowed over to the captured passenger ship. After a short conversation all the passengers and crew were ordered to abandon ship. The Carolina was to be destroyed.

According to survivor's testimony, first women and children then all others took to the ten lifeboats and rowed away from the doomed vessel. They watched helplessly as the German submarine, U-151 shot four times just below the water line and the Carolina slowly sank.

There were no casualties as a result of the sinking by the U-151, however, during the night, as those in the lifeboats rowed toward the shore, a storm struck. Forty-eight people drowned when their lifeboats were upset.

Today the Carolina lies approximately 65 miles off Beach Haven Inlet. Although her remains are often fished for cod and pollack, few divers have ventured deep enough to see the wreckage. Thus, little is known about the condition of her structure and what artifacts remain. Due to the depth, it is likely to stay this way.

Cayru, courtesy of the U.S. Coast Guard.

CAYRU

BUILT: 1919
VESSEL TYPE: FREIGHTER
LENGTH: 390 FEET

LOST: MARCH 8, 1942
DEPTH: 120 TO 130 FEET
LOCATION: 26724.5/42963.0
(GALIMORE'S CAYRU)

The 5,152 gross ton Brazilian freighter Cayru was on a northerly course when a torpedo suddenly struck her amidships. The ship began sinking immediately and all those aboard took to lifeboats. While rowing away from the doomed vessel, the lifeboats were approached by a U-boat that surfaced nearby. The German sailors requested information about the Cayru and wanted to know if everyone had abandoned ship. Once assured that the vessel was vacant, the U-boat circled back and sent another torpedo into the side of the stricken ship. She went quickly to the bottom, and to this day has not been located.

Many fishermen and divers have searched for her watery grave. During these searches numerous other shipwrecks have been discovered. One is known as "Galimore's Cayru." Found over ten years ago by a sea captain named Skip Galimore of the Barnegat area, it was mistakenly thought to be the Brazilian freighter. After a few dives on the scattered remains, it was determined by the age of the artifacts recovered that it could not be the torpedoed Cayru. "Galimore's Cayru" sank sometime in the late 1800s.

The "Galimore's Cayru" is located southwest of the R.P. Resor and like the Resor, is considered an excellent shark fishing wreck. Because it is dove so infrequently, there are still many artifacts being recovered. Hopefully, the identity of "Galimore's Cayru" will someday be uncovered and the location of the actual Cayru will be revealed.

Chaparra, courtesy of The Steamship Historical Society, University of Baltimore Library.

CHAPARRA

BUILT: 1906
VESSEL TYPE: FREIGHTER
LENGTH: 249 FEET

LOST: OCTOBER 27, 1918
DEPTH: 80 FEET
LOCATION: 26847.6/43239.9

The Cuban steamship Chaparra sank in less than ten minutes when it struck a mine laid by a German submarine. Six men were killed in the incident and thirteen made it to safety with the assistance of the Coast Guard.

No submarine was seen in the area, but the manner in which the ship sank caused officials to believe it was a mine. The sinking occurred about five miles from the spot where the Mallory Line freighter, San Saba, had struck a mine just eighteen days prior.

The Chaparra, 249.5 feet in length and of 1,600 gross tons registry, was loaded with 2,000 tons of sugar, consigned to the Federal Sugar Refining Company in New York.

The remains of the freighter rest today in 80 feet of water, eight miles off Barnegat Inlet. The site is often visited by boats sailing from the Barnegat Inlet because of its popularity among local divers. The steel wreckage rises 25 feet from the bottom and can be easily penetrated in many areas. Many large lobster and blackfish have been taken from this wreck. When scheduling a dive on this wreck, plan to do a little fishing for the overly abundant blackfish. Fresh fish and lobster make a great menu combination!

Charlemagne Tower, Jr., courtesy of The Steamship Historical Society, University of Baltimore Library.

CHARLEMAGNE TOWER, JR.

BUILT: 1888
VESSEL TYPE: GREAT LAKE
  ORE SHIP
LENGTH: 255 FEET

LOST: MARCH 6, 1914
DEPTH: 55 FEET
LOCATION: 26912.8/43339.2

Better known as the "Cedar Creek Wreck," the 1,825 gross ton Charlemagne Tower, Jr. laid in mothballs for about six years before her final voyage. She was in need of an overhaul and her owners were looking for a quick fix. In February 1914 repair work was complete and she was recommissioned.

On March 4, 1914, Captain H.C. Simmons and a crew of 18 set sail from Norfolk, Virginia to Boston, Massachusetts with a cargo of coal. After traveling only a few hours, engine trouble was experienced and Captain Simmons decided to head back to port for the necessary repairs. Once the problems were corrected, the Charlemagne Tower, Jr. again headed out to sea.

South of Barnegat and a few miles offshore, the ore ship began taking on water for no apparent reason. Captain Simmons gave the order to head toward shore, into shallower waters. By morning on March 6, 1914 her seams completely opened and the Great Lake ore carrier filled with water to the upper deck causing her engines and all electronics to shut down.

When the captain gave the order to abandon ship, the crew launched the lifeboats and rowed the mile to shore. By that time the Life Saving crew from the Cedar Creek Station had also launched a boat. Unfortunately the surf was too rough and they could only assist from shore. By nightfall all the crew members from the Charlemagne Tower, Jr. had been rescued.

Today the "Cedar Creek Wreck" is, unfortunately, often overlooked. Just a few miles from the Barnegat Inlet, this is an excellent second dive site, or a place to stop and fish awhile before quitting for the day. The wreckage lies only a few feet off the bottom, but can easily be found because of its size. School size seabass in large numbers inhabit the area. Cunners and blackfish also make up a large population. From a diving perspective, few artifacts have been found but legal size lobster are often taken.

Edgar F. Lukenbach, later to be recommissioned the USS Cherokee.

USS CHEROKEE

BUILT: 1891
VESSEL TYPE: USS PATROL
  BOAT
LENGTH: 120 FEET

LOST: FEBRUARY 26, 1918
DEPTH: 110 FEET
LOCATION: 26982.0/42519.1

The USS Cherokee, also known as the "Gun Boat", was built in 1891 and was originally christened the Edgar F. Lukenbach serving as a tug, towing barges. The Lukenbach was towing two schooner barges, the A.G. Ropes and Undaunted, with loads of coal during a winter gale. She couldn't keep up with her tow and had to cut the schooner barges free. Unfortunately both vessels wrecked and many of the crew were lost. The tug searched for the missing crew members and then returned to port.

On October 12, 1917 the U.S. Navy obtained the tug and two months later she was recommissioned as the USS Cherokee.

On February 24, 1918 fully supplied with three inch deck guns the Cherokee left New London, Connecticut for Washington, D.C. with six officers and thirty-three crewmen. At 7:00 p.m., February 25, 1918 the patrol boat passed the Barnegat whistle buoy under clear skies, cruising at 9.3 knots. At 8:00 p.m. the radioman received an advisory storm warning predicting strong southwest gales. By 12:00 a.m. on the 26th, the Cherokee was on a southerly course encountering heavy seas. Throughout the night the seas poured into the vessel's hatches and the pumps fought to keep up with the incoming water. By 7:00 a.m. the wind had shifted to the west and an attempt to change course toward safe harbor proved to be the death of the patrol boat. The steering gear broke and the helmsman aboard couldn't maneuver the ship to approach the oncoming waves. As a result the Cherokee foundered taking twenty-nine of her crewmen with her.

According to diver Joe Milligan the "Gun Boat" lies in just 100 feet of water. The hull is still intact and its large props are under the stern. A large deck gun is still on the bow covered with growth. Artifacts that have been recovered from the wreck site include 3-inch shells, machine gun ammo, four large brass capstans, silverware and nautical items. Plenty of fish reside on the wreck as well. One fish of interest that appeared to make the wreck his permanent residence was a large drum fish. Other fish include tog, black seabass, and on occasion, monk fish.

CHINA JUNK WRECK

VESSEL TYPE: SCHOONER
DEPTH: 15 FEET
CONSTRUCTION: METAL
LOCATION: 27062.9/42866.7

Approximately one mile out of Townsend Inlet, off the shore of Avalon, New Jersey lie the remains of a schooner. Located just west of the bell buoy, the scattered wreckage is lying low to the ocean floor. Some believe that the wreck received her name from the china recovered from the site. Others believe the vessel lying beneath the waves was a vessel from China which had been reported lost October 4, 1875, in the vicinity of the "China Wreck."

The wreck is almost never dove because of the strong inlet currents and poor visibility. It is, however, fished by anglers who drift in the area of the bell buoy. Fishermen need not have their depth recorder on to know when they are upon the wreck. It is apparent by the number of seabass and porgies that seem to instantly appear. The action is non-stop. Weakfish, fluke, blues and blackfish are also caught while drifting in this area. In fact, it was reported by a local bait and tackle shop that even striped bass are occasionally caught on the "China Junk Wreck."

CHINA WRECK

VESSEL TYPE: CARGO VESSEL
DEPTH: 39 FEET
CONSTRUCTION: WOOD
LOCATION: 27098.0/42658.3

Off the coast of New Jersey lie hundreds if not thousands of shipwrecks yet to be discovered. There are an equal number of vessels that have been found but never identified. One such wreck is known as the "China Wreck."

This unidentified wreck was discovered in the early 1970s by two wire dragging ships, the Rude and the Heck. They were assigned to the Delaware Bay and its entrance with a mission to survey underwater obstructions that could be possible hazards to navigation.

Once a hazard was located, divers would explore the obstruction to determine whether or not it was necessary to reduce it for safe navigating. This was done by dragging a heavy wire between the two vessels catching the obstacle in their path and leveling it to an exceptable depth.

While dragging just southeast of Cape May, the wire caught an obstruction and the divers suited up. They proceeded down the line to investigate the snag. Commander Merritt N. Walter, who was on that historical dive, remembered it as follows:

"We slowly followed the ground wire to the bottom toward the obstruction. Laying next to the wire we spotted an exposed dish, partly covered with coral. A few feet from it we found another, and still another. Then we saw it, looming up out of the haze like an apparition, sort of shadowy and spooky. It looked like a pile of debris. It was eight to ten feet high and about thirty feet across. A closer look revealed all kinds of cups and saucers, bowls, pitchers and every kind of chinaware.

"Beyond this pile the rest of the wreck laid open, exposing thousands of neatly packed British-made chinaware. And when I say thousands, I mean thousands! It looked like some kind of bargain basement sale at Macy's with all the stuff stacked there waiting for shoppers. That is when I signaled my partner topside."

Today the "China Wreck" lies 7.5 miles off Cape May in 39 feet of water. Fortunately for divers and fishermen, the wreck was left as originally found. Although much of its cargo has been recovered over the years, china is still brought up by those willing to search. Because the wreckage is very scattered and at its highest peak only rises five feet off the bottom, marine life here consists mainly of smaller fish, clams and scallops.

Choapa, courtesy of the U.S. Coast Guard.

CHOAPA

BUILT: 1937
VESSEL TYPE: FREIGHTER
LENGTH: 292 FEET

LOST: SEPTEMBER 21, 1944
DEPTH: 200 FEET
LOCATION: 26832.5/43549.5

During World War II, German U-boats made merchant shipping unsafe and uneasy. To help deter the attacks of the Wolfpacks, merchant vessels often traveled in convoys.

On the fog shrouded night of September 20th, the Choapa, fifth in a convoy of seven, collided with the British tanker Harmony. A total of five vessels were involved in the collision, but none were seriously damaged. The skipper of the Choapa choose to anchor and wait for the fog to lift so he could investigate the damage. The next day the tanker Voco, approaching the channel to New York, hit the Choapa while she was still at anchor. Yet another vessel, the Empire Garrick, also struck the ill-fated ship and sent her to the bottom, stern first. The Voco was not seriously impaired and stood by to render assistance by taking the crew of the Choapa aboard.

Located approximately 12 miles offshore Asbury Park on the eastern edge of the Mud Hole, the 1,700 gross ton freighter remains intact but badly deteriorated, facing east in a 150 feet of water. The wreck can be reached at 100 feet and makes for good diving. Like most wrecks located in the area of the Mud Hole, the visibility can range from 0 to 100 feet. According to diver Joe Milligan the wreck of Choapa is not a great lobster wreck but an occasional bug is captured. The wreck is considered a good nautical artifact wreck.

City of Athens

CITY OF ATHENS

BUILT: 1911
VESSEL TYPE: PASSENGER
   FREIGHTER
LENGTH: 309 FEET

LOST: MAY 1, 1918
DEPTH: 105 FEET
LOCATION: 26920.3/42705.3

On the fog shrouded morning of May 1, 1918, the Savannah Line steamer, City of Athens, was rammed by the French naval cruiser La Glorie. The 309 foot coastal, passenger freighter was traveling with no navigational lights due to "black out" regulations imposed by the United States government during the war. The investigating officials determined that the cause of the accident was due to the heavy morning fog and the lack of navigational lights.

Because the collision occurred early in the morning, most of the 135 passengers and crew on board were below deck asleep. This resulted in a loss of 68 lives.

Today the remains of the City of Athens lie in 110 feet of water. The wreck rises 50 feet off the ocean floor. Diver Joe Milligan from Lansdowne, Pennsylvania who has dove the wreck more than 200 times describes it best. "An antique store under water." Joe commented that the wreckage lists to the port 10 to 20 degrees. Some of the artifacts recovered were; rifles, dishes, magnolia bars, beer bottles, ammunition, oil bottles and various nautical artifacts.

CITY OF GEORGETOWN

BUILT: 1902
VESSEL TYPE: WOODEN
  SCHOONER
LENGTH: 170 FEET

LOST: FEBRUARY 2, 1913
DEPTH: 112 FEET
LOCATION: 26980.3/42461.5

The 559 gross ton City of Georgetown left the safe harbor of New York on a southerly course toward Savannah, Georgia with a cargo of sugar. Her captain, A.J. Slocum, had sailed the four masted schooner since she was put into service in 1902.

Having no elaborate navigational equipment, the captain steered his vessel close to the coast using landmarks and buoys to identify locations. On the night of February 2, 1913, one of the landmarks that usually assisted in his navigation would be the chief contributor to the demise of the schooner.

The helmsman and lookout, checking their charts, noted that they were coming upon the Five Fathom Lightship. Observing this they were able to pinpoint their location at the mouth of the Delaware Bay just south of Cape May. This information was logged just after midnight.

At approximately the same hour, the Hamburg-American steamship Prinz Oskar had just cleared the Delaware Breakwater and had came upon the Five Fathom Lightship. The Prinz Osker positioned herself to begin her journey across the Atlantic. Unknown to her helmsmen, hidden by the bright beacon of the lightship, the City of Georgetown sailed silently toward them.

As the Prinz Oskar made her way around the lightship a lookout spotted the much smaller vessel on a collision course. The two vessels were so close, however, there was no time to react and take emergency action. The bow of the schooner hit the port bow of the steamship with such a violent collision its wooden bow sprit pierced the steel plating and held the two ships together as one.

In an effort to save his vessel from sinking, the captain of the Prinz Oskar ordered his engines reversed and freed his ship from the fatally wounded schooner. Immediately the City of Georgetown started to go down by the bow. All eight crew members aboard the sinking schooner were rescued by the crew on the Oskar.

According to diver Joe Milligan, the remains of the schooner lie at a depth of 112 feet. The main wreckage is in three separate pieces. Each section lies low to the sand and consists mainly of her wooden deck. Joe considers the wreck to be a "typical lobster snag." He also commented that plenty of seabass, tog, ling and eel pouts inhabit the site.

A lucky catch by the author while diving on a "lobster snag". This 20 pounder will turn a lot of heads at the dock.

Coimbra, courtesy of the U.S. Coast Guard.

COIMBRA

BUILT: UNKNOWN
VESSEL TYPE: OIL TANKER
LENGTH: 423 FEET

LOST: JANUARY 15, 1942
DEPTH: 180 FEET
LOCATION: 26204.0/43576.3

During times of war, reports of casualties at sea are often censored and depend primarily on survivor testimony. Such is the case with the Coimbra. The 6,770 gross ton British tanker was approximately thirty miles off Moriches Inlet when she was struck without warning by three torpedoes from the German submarine U-123. The tanker cargo of fuel oil ignited with the torpedoes' explosion and immediately the flaming ship began to sink. Of the forty-four crew members on board, only ten lived to tell of their horrifying January 15, 1942 ordeal.

Today the wreck of the Coimbra lies in 180 feet of water rising 40 to 60 feet off the ocean floor. It is an excellent dive site for experienced deep divers. Many nautical artifacts have been recovered.

Fishing over the wreckage during the summer months can yield nearly every species of north Atlantic fish. Fish often caught include cod, tog, black seabass, ling, sole, pollack and hake. Swimming over the wreck in search of a meal are blues, striped bass, tuna and shark. When fishing the Coimbra beware that she is broken into three main pieces. Most of the fish tend to concentrate where the wreckage lies broken and close to the sand.

Continent, courtesy of the U.S. Coast Guard.

CONTINENT

BUILT: 1921
VESSEL TYPE: FREIGHTER
LENGTH: 149 FEET

LOST: JANUARY 10, 1942
DEPTH: 130 FEET
LOCATION: 26884.7/43637.4

A month after the collision between the Continent and Byron D. Benson, the Department of Commerce, Bureau of Marine Inspection and Navigation, issued a ruling on the cause. It was determined that the Continent, a 468 gross ton, single engine screw freighter, was at fault for neglecting to have competent persons in charge of navigation duties, on the bridge, prior to and at the time of the collision.

The report showed that both vessels had a lookout, each of who spotted the other vessel. It was also indicated that the seas as being rough but the night was relatively clear.

The Byron D. Benson, carrying a cargo of crude oil, bound for New York from Texas, was the much larger vessel weighing 7,953 gross tons. Since the Benson, having the right of way, kept its course and maintained speed until it determined the Continent was taking no action to avoid a collision. The Byron D. Benson's crew sounded one blast of his horn and changed course in attempt to steer clear of the oncoming Continent. Only after this evasive action did those aboard the freighter react, but by then it was too late.

The 465 foot tanker delivered such a blow to the Continent that the smaller vessel went down almost immediately. Of the fourteen man crew aboard, one lost his life in the incident. The other thirteen crew members were picked up by lifeboats from the Benson.

Today, the scattered remains of the Continent lie in 130 feet of water in the vicinity of the "BA" buoy. She is approximately 9.2 miles east of the Sandy Hook Channel in the 17 fathom area. Not many dive boats visit her remains due to the location. She rests on a silt bottom and the visibility is usually poor. The anglers I spoke to who fish the wreck said it holds seabass, blackfish, ling and summer flounder.

Creole, courtesy of The Mariners Museum, Newport News, Virginia.

CREOLE

BUILT: 1862
VESSEL TYPE: COASTAL
  STEAMER
LENGTH: APPROX. 200 FEET

LOST: MARCH 17, 1868
DEPTH: 20 FEET
LOCATION: 200 FEET OFF
  JETTY AT BAY HEAD

Before the implementation of the Life Saving Stations in the 1800s, documentation of shipping disasters was inadequate and performed intermittently. Therefore, little is known about the 1868 demise of the Creole.

A photograph shows that the vessel was approximately 200 feet in length and was used as a coastal steamer. From dubious reports and one survivor's testimony, it is surmised that she ran aground off the beach in Bay Head.

Today, it is believed that the broken remains of a steamer lying in 20 feet of water off the beach of the old Bay Head Hotel are those of the Creole. Although the name of this vessel has never been positively identified, its description is consistent with that of the steamer. The wreckage is scattered over a large area and consists of steel hull plates, machinery, boilers and decking.

Although unconfirmed, one diver claims to have taken a large anchor from the wreck. Many small fish and lobster inhabit the site. Her remains are great for a beach dive since she is loaded with artifacts for those who dig deep enough. In the fall, fishing over the Creole has been rewarding, especially for bluefish patrolling up and down the beach.

S.S. DELAWARE

BUILT: 1880
VESSEL TYPE: PASSENGER
   FREIGHTER
LENGTH: 250 FEET

LOST: JULY 9, 1898
DEPTH: 70 FEET
LOCATION: 26928.4/43467.5

The Clyde Line steamer Delaware, left Pier 29 of New York's East River at 3:30 p.m. on Friday, July 1, 1898. At approximately 9:30 that evening, five miles north of Barnegat Light and five miles offshore, a fire was discovered in the hold. The crew and male passengers aboard immediately tried to extinguish the blaze with the water hoses, but the fire proved to be too much. When the situation became hopeless, Captain A.D. Ingram, a sea captain of 21 years with the Clyde Line organization, ordered the lowering of lifeboats and began preparations for abandoning ship.

The fire attracted other boats in the area and also gained the attention of Life Saving Station Keeper Brinkley of Station 15. Known as the Cedar Creek Station, it is still standing today on the grounds of Island Beach State Park. Keeper Brinkley and his men put out their boats and were on the scene immediately. There were no casualties. Captain Ingram, his crewmen and all passengers were taken to the Cedar Creek Station where they were given dry clothes, food and drink.

The vessel itself drifted up the beach with the current and sank off Bay Head, New Jersey on Saturday, July 2nd at approximately 4:30 p.m. Cargo and vessel were a total loss.

The Delaware had been used for years as a freighter but the government took over the rights to the ship and refitted it as a troop transport/passenger ship. Built in Philadelphia, Pennsylvania by the firm of Birgey, Hillman and Streaker in 1880, the Delaware was constructed of oak yellow pine with iron and copper fastenings. She was valued at $125,000 and registered at 1,279 gross tons. The vessel was 251.5 feet long, 17.5 deep and had a beam of 37 feet.

Today many divers up and down the East Coast visit the wreck of the Delaware each year. The remains lie in 67 feet of water approximately 1.5 miles off Bay Head. There is a abundance of marine life that inhabit the wreck during the summer months. Artifacts are still recovered from the wreck by those who spend the time to sift the sand. In the fall of 1989, diver Joe Paola and the author recovered the ship's bell.

S.S. Delaware, photo by Mike Sonta.

Delaware, underwater drawing by Al Hoffman and M. Colasurdo.

**Big yellowfin and bluefin tuna can usually be found around the ''Bacardi Wreck.''
Photo by Pete Barrett.**

DURLEY CHINE (BACARDI WRECK)

BUILT: 1913
VESSEL TYPE: FREIGHTER
LENGTH: 279 FEET

LOST: APRIL 22, 1917
DEPTH: 110 FEET
LOCATION: 26308.1/43310.6

The Durley Chine, known locally as the "Bacardi" was traveling in ballast from Nova Scotia, to Virginia when she encountered the British steamer, Harlem. The 1,918 gross ton Durley Chine was built in 1913 by Osbourne, Grahm & Co., Sunderland, England and was owned by the Canadian Government. Powered by coal-fired steam, her dimensions were 279 feet by 40 feet by 18 feet.

At approximately 1:30 a.m. while sailing under the cover of darkness, the Harlem and Durley Chine collided. Almost immediately, the Durley Chine was sent to the bottom, taking the entire crew of twenty-eight into the water. The Harlem, badly damaged but afloat, was able to rescue all the crewmen from the Durley Chine. Then, without assistance, the Harlem was able to limp into New York.

For over thirty years the "Bacardi Wreck" has been well known to fishermen and divers. She received her nickname from a Long Island charter boat captain, after fishing the wreck the first time. The anglers aboard experienced such great success they planned a second excursion trip the next day. To mark the wreck for the next trip a float was needed. The story goes that one of the regulars, who was known more for his drinking than fishing, willingly gave up his empty bottle of Bacardi Rum to be used as the marker, hence the name "Bacardi Wreck."

Located at the 30 fathom mark she is a haven for tuna and shark fishermen alike. Her real name was revealed only a few years ago when a diver recovered the ship's bell and the Durley Chine's true identity became known.

The wreckage of the Durley Chine lies north to northeast. The stern section is mostly intact and rises high above the sand. The hull just forward of the stern, is mostly broken up. This is where divers report the greatest concentration of large blackfish, seabass and lobster. The midsection of the wreck, engines and boiler area also rises high off the ocean floor. More exploration is needed in this area. The bow of the Durley Chine is mostly intact and lies over on its side.

Edward H. Cole, photo by John Raguso.

EDWARD H. COLE

BUILT: 1904
VESSEL TYPE: FOUR MASTED
  SCHOONER
LENGTH: 228 FEET

LOST: JUNE 2, 1918
DEPTH: 185 FEET
LOCATION: 26536.2/42853.7

On June 2, 1918, the date known as "Black Sunday," the German submarine fleet sank a total of 11 merchant ships. One of the unfortunate victims was the Edward H. Cole. The four masted, three decked schooner was built in 1904 in Rockland, Maine. She was 228 feet in length with a gross weight of 1,791 tons.

Bound for Portland, Maine from Norfolk, Virginia, the ship was traveling slowly under a light northwesterly wind. It was almost four in the afternoon when a submarine was spotted surfacing a half mile off the port bow. After circling the schooner three times, an officer on the deck of the U-boat requested information about the vessel. As the U-boat neared the Cole, a small dingy with an officer and three crewmen boarded and inspected the vessel. The U-boat officer gave the crew of the Cole ten minutes to abandon ship before he would destroy the schooner.

As the nine crewmen aboard the schooner lowered their lifeboat and rowed away from the doomed vessel, they watched in disbelief as the men from the U-boat attached bombs just above the waterline and sank the Edward H. Cole.

No sooner had the vessel settled below the surface, when the U-boat turned and with full steam ahead, was in pursuit of a merchant vessel sighted on the horizon. An hour later, the crew of the Cole watched a small tanker sinking by the stern. The U-boat had claimed yet another victim.

Today, the schooner lies on the bottom in 180 feet of water. Divers who have made the 50 mile boat ride to the site say that it is one of the best dives in New Jersey. It is asserted that the wreck is everything a diver wants; good spearfishing, excellent photography, big lobster and plenty of treasure for the artifact seekers.

Year-round, the wreck of the Edward H. Cole is a fish producer. Local fishermen venture out to the area in the spring and fall of the year in pursuit of cod, haddock and pollack. During the late summer months the wreck is fished for tuna and shark. Year-round blackfish, seabass and ling inhabit the wreck.

EUGENE F. MORAN

BUILT: 1902
VESSEL TYPE: TUG BOAT
LENGTH: 91 FEET

LOST: DECEMBER 9, 1917
DEPTH: 25 FEET
LOCATION: 26939.0/43022.2

The 91 foot steel-hulled tug boat Eugene F. Moran was built in 1902 at the Neane & Levy Ship Yard, Philadelphia, Pennsylvania. On Sunday morning, December 9, 1917, the tug and its tow of two pile drivers, were proceeding north in a terrific sixty mile an hour gale. The tug was struggling to make headway against the raging storm. Realizing he could no longer proceed north, captain Frederick Riley decided to cut loose his tow and return to the work barges to rescue the crew of two on each. However, as the tug headed south she ran onto the sandbar off Atlantic City and struck a submerged wreck. The Eugene F. Moran went to the bottom, bow first, in a matter of seconds, taking all eleven crew members with her.

Life Saving crews from Atlantic City and Long Port watched as the tug struggled with her tow, expecting trouble in the raging storm. As the two work barges tossed helplessly, the men of the Life Saving Stations put out in their lifeboats to lend whatever assistance they could. The larger of the two barges struck the sandbar, its deck immediately awash by the pounding surf. The lighter barge cleared the sandbar, drifted through the inlet and washed ashore on Mankiller Island. All four men aboard the barges were rescued by the men of the Life Saving Stations.

Today, the wreck of the Eugene F. Moran lies on the Atlantic City sandbar in 30 feet of water. The tug no longer resembles a ship since she was demolished for safe navigation. The Moran is not visited often, but those who dive the wreck report that many weakfish inhabit the area in late summer and that it is a "hot spot" of the local bottom fishermen.

EVENING STAR

BUILT: UNKNOWN   **LOST:** UNKNOWN
VESSEL TYPE: TANKER   **DEPTH:** 40 FEET
LENGTH: UNKNOWN   **LOCATION:** 27032.1/42760.9

The demise of the tanker Evening Star isn't found in any history books. Like many ships lost in World War II, much of the news about her sinking was censored and never released to the public. Her name may be that of her registration or just a symbol to identify the remains of an unknown tanker.

Better known as the "Pig Iron Wreck" she is popular to bottom fishermen who sail out of Cape May. The scattered remains cover a large area of the bottom in 40 feet of water about 12 miles off Cape May Inlet. Black seabass, tog and fluke are caught while fishing over the wreckage. Drifting around the area of the Evening Star has been productive for bluefish and weakfish.

From a diving standpoint, visibility is often fair to poor with the wreckage lying low to the bottom. Few lobster inhabit the wreck, possibly due to the depth. As for artifacts, there have only been a few portholes and cage lanterns recovered.

FALL RIVER

BUILT: 1911
VESSEL TYPE: BARGE
LENGTH: APPROX. 200 FEET

LOST: NOVEMBER 1, 1932
DEPTH: 70 FEET
LOCATION: 26898.1/42984.2

The wreck of the barge, Fall River, received little attention from the news media since there was no loss of life and the cargo of coal had little monetary value. Today, however, she is noted as an excellent fishing location, and is often referred to as the "Brigantine Buoy Wreck" or the "AC Barge Wreck."

According to a New York Times article at the time of the sinking, the tug Eureka (which later sank off Long Island) was towing three coal barges north to Boston for the Martin Corporation. For no apparent reason the 1,759 gross ton Fall River split her seams and began taking on water. The crew of four aboard the barge manned the pumps and attempted to keep her afloat. The tug, Eureka, changed course and headed toward shore in an effort to bring her tow aground. The next day, only a few miles off Absecon, New Jersey, the vessel appeared to be lost. The crew of the barge were removed for safety by the Atlantic City Coast Guard. Soon after the barge was cut free and she sank beneath the surface. Because the Fall River was a navigational hazard she was demolished and now rises only ten feet off the bottom.

The splintered remains of the barge lie approximately eight miles east of Absecon Inlet. The wooden wreckage rises five to ten feet above the sandy bottom and is an excellent fishing spot. Diving the wreck has always produced lobster, although not that easily. The wreckage provides deep holes in which the lobster hide, so a lobster hook is required.

FATUK

BUILT: UNKNOWN   **LOST:** OCTOBER 27, 1988
VESSEL TYPE: FISH FREIGHTER   **DEPTH:** 80 FEET
LENGTH: 166 FEET   **LOCATION:** 26871.7/43196.1

With the aid of sophisticated navigational equipment and weather tracking systems, the likelihood of a modern day disaster at sea is unlikely. Seeing the chance to help mother nature, artificial reef programs have been adopted up and down the Atlantic seaboard. With the efforts of many organizations, including the New Jersey Wildlife Management and The Fisherman Magazine, six artificial reefs have been created off the New Jersey coast. One of the ships placed on the Garden State North Reef is the Fatuk.

Although the demise of the Fatuk was planned, how she became the custody of the United States Government is quite a story. Disguised as a commercial fishing vessel, the 166 foot freighter was registered to the Panamanian government.

The Fatuk's crew was off-loading her catch of fish in New Bedford, Massachusetts. Because the ship was poorly maintained, she attracted the attention of the customs officials. On two separate occasions she was boarded and inspected but no apparent wrongdoing was cited. When the customs officials boarded the Fatuk for the third time, the decision was made to cut open some of the frozen fish. Upon doing so they found over 52,000 pounds of marijuana.

For our benefit today, the Fatuk was donated to the artificial reef fund. After much hard work and numerous donations, she was towed to her resting place, her seacocks opened and she sank to the bottom.

Today, the wreck resembles other ships that have been on the bottom for many years. She is covered with aquatic growth, barnacles and mussels. The wreck is located in 80 feet of water approximately eight miles northeast of Beach Haven Inlet. The wreck is fully intact and now home for many fish. Few lobster have been spotted, probably due to the lack of hiding places. There are an abundance of seabass in the hold, with bergal and cunners circling the area as if protecting the Fatuk.

Fortuna, the only remains of the Italian bark on the beach at Ship Bottom.

FORTUNA

BUILT: 1869
VESSEL TYPE: THREE MASTED
  BARK
LENGTH: 193 FEET

LOST: JANUARY 18, 1910
DEPTH: 0 FEET
LOCATION: 16TH STREET,
  SHIP BOTTOM

The Italian bark, Fortuna, was bound for New York carrying a cargo of coal. Those aboard included Captain Luigi Andragna, his wife and three children, and thirteen crewmen.

As is typical during the winter months along the Jersey coast, the weather was ominous. The Fortuna was being driven in a north-westerly direction by a winter storm. Fog, rain and high seas made it difficult for Captain Andragna to determine his position. With little warning, the tossing ship came to an abrupt halt as it hit ground, just offshore of what is now known as Ship Bottom, New Jersey.

The vessel, aground and within sight of the local Life Saving Station, caught the immediate attention of station Captain Ike Truex. The Life Saving crew was summoned and all aboard were removed without incident. The intent was to wait for the next high tide to pull the Fortuna from the sand. The wrecking steamer, Relief, was dispatched to tow her out to sea.

Unfortunately, the seas ran even higher the following day, dis-banding any salvage plans and driving the bark harder into the shore. As the tide subsided, the water that was supporting her in an upright position could no longer do so, and the 983 ton, iron-hulled vessel rolled over with her bottom facing the beach. This is how the town of Ship Bottom got its famous name, so the legend goes.

As she was torn apart in the storm, beachcombers carried away all that was salvageable. The little that was left was eventually buried beneath the sand at Sixteenth Street. The anchor of the Fortuna was recently retrieved by a group of local residents, and is now on display at the borough hall.

The G & D Wreck offers a mixed variety of species from huge bluefish to sharks and cod to dolphin. Photo by Pete Barrett.

GLORIA & DORIS (G&D WRECK)

VESSEL TYPE: STEAMSHIP
DEPTH: 110 FEET
CONSTRUCTION: STEEL HULL
LOCATION: 26671.2/43572.7

The Gloria & Doris was first discovered by a charter boat captain fishing in the area. Since the identity of the wreck was unknown, the captain named her after the only two female patrons aboard, Gloria and Doris. The wreck is more commonly known as the G&D Wreck.

Vessels traveling out of Fire Island, New York will find the wreck located almost 25 miles south of the inlet. For those leaving out of Sandy Hook, the trip is approximately 35 miles offshore.

The G&D Wreck rests with its bow facing north, intact and listing to the port. The bow rises twenty feet off the bottom and is the most attractive to divers. They can penetrate this section and often find large lobster inside. Moving aft, you will see a low lying area covered by sand. Continuing on, you will come to decking and steel hull plates. This part is yet unexplored by divers, although a few portholes have been recovered.

Still moving aft you will reach the boilers and engine. Many brass nautical artifacts have been taken from this section. In addition the largest concentration of fish are located in this region. Ling and cod inhabit the wreck year-round. Bluefish, tuna, skipjack, bonito, dolphin and sharks are often found cruising the Gloria & Doris during the warmer months. The stern is low to the sand and is broken up. This too, is relatively unexplored territory. Visibility is usually excellent, often exceeding forty feet.

Great Isaac, courtesy of Steve Lang, Tug Boat Photo Research.

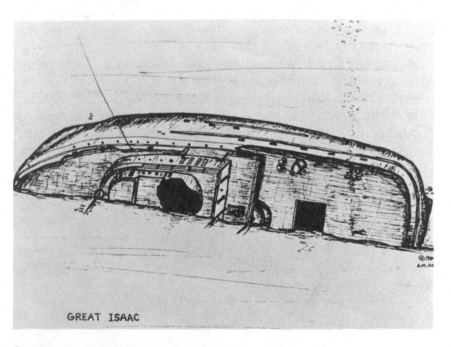

Great Isaac, underwater drawing by Al Hoffman.

GREAT ISAAC

BUILT: 1944
VESSEL TYPE: TUG
LENGTH: 185 FEET

LOST: APRIL 16, 1947
DEPTH: 90 FEET
LOCATION: 26840.9/43195.2

The Great Isaac sank in a matter of minutes when she collided with the Norwegian freighter Bandeirante. The single screw, oceangoing tug, with a crew of 27, was towing the liberty ship, Thomas M. Cooley, from the naval yard in Norfolk, Virginia to New York. Just south of Barnegat, New Jersey, a dense fog and very rough seas were encountered. Skipper Ernest McCreary said he gave the order to sound the foghorn when he heard another ship's foghorn in the distance. This occurred approximately five miles south of the Barnegat Lightship.

The Bandeirante emerged suddenly from the dense fog and struck the tug amidship on the port side, driving six feet into the engine room. The Great Isaac was sinking fast when the order was given to abandon ship. All 27 crewmen were rescued with no serious injuries, but the Isaac was lost. Considered one of the better dives in New Jersey waters, the wreck is completely intact, resting in almost 90 feet of water. The Isaac shows very little sign of deterioration. She is lying with her port side buried in the sand and the rounded hull making up a large part of the wreckage. The ship is easily penetrated, but penetration lines are recommended. Many artifacts have been taken from the Great Isaac, however, a few portholes do remain. On the hull, you will find blankets of large mussels, and surrounding the wreck are plenty of large seabass and blackfish. The wreck is a favorite and can be dove by both the novice and expert.

Gulf Trade, courtesy of the U.S. Coast Guard.

GULF TRADE

BUILT: 1920
VESSEL TYPE: TANKER
LENGTH: 430 FEET

LOST: MARCH 10, 1942
DEPTH: BOW 60 FEET
LOCATION: 26889.2/43263.5
STERN: 90 FEET 26821.3/43318.3

The 430 foot, Gulf Trade, was bound for New York from Port Author, Texas, when it was struck by a torpedo. Loaded with over 80,000 gallons of fuel oil, the tanker sank off Barnegat Light, New Jersey; another war casualty.

With rough seas and oncoming ship traffic, Captain Torgen Olsen made the fatal mistake of ordering the flashing of the ship's running lights to avoid a collision. Only minutes after his decision, the wolfpack's bite was felt as a torpedo ripped the Gulf Trade amidship, splitting her completely in two. Both sections were instantly engulfed in flames but were quickly extinguished as the heavy seas and strong winds rolled over both halves of the stricken tanker.

Eighteen crewmen in the forward section took to a lifeboat but were never seen again. The captain and six other crewmen on the stern section boarded a second lifeboat. Nine others chose to remain on the floating overturned stern section awaiting assistance. The captain and the men with him were picked up by a rescue vessel as were the remaining survivors on the stern.

The stern floated east of Barnegat Inlet and finally sank. The bow drifted within five miles of shore and ran aground, where a partial salvage of the oil was performed.

Today, the Gulf Trade lies in two sections some eight miles apart. The bow section lies 4.5 miles east of Barnegat Inlet and rests in 54 feet of water. The stern section is some 13 miles northeast of the Barnegat Inlet and rests fully intact on the bottom with 80 feet of water over her remains. The stern rises 35 feet off the bottom and is dove more often than the demolished bow section.

Sea life is abundant on both sections of the Gulf Trade, but the stern is a better fishing location than the bow. During the spring run of whiting and ling, charter boats from Barnegat frequent the wreck for good fishing. In the warmer months both sections are overrun with blackfish and seabass. One of the largest concentration of headfish ever reported by a diver was spotted on the stern section. There were more than 100 all weighing over 25 pounds.

A diver's delight. While diving the Hankins Wreck, Howard Rothweiler captured this five and a half pound lobster. Photo by Tom Nolan.

HANKINS WRECK

VESSEL TYPE: UNKNOWN
DEPTH: 80 FEET
CONSTRUCTION: WOOD
LOCATION: 26884.5/43340.6

A few miles inshore from the wreck of the Tolten, lie unidentified remains known as the Hankins Wreck. The wreckage is in large sections, low to the bottom. They appear to be mostly decking with the structure buried beneath the sand. Plenty of holes make the decaying remains an excellent lobster snag. Many large lobster of more than five pounds have appeared on the dinner table as a result of a day's dive at the Hankins Wreck.

Fishing the Hankins has produced coolers loaded with ling for skillful anglers. Ling inhabit the wreck year-round and make up the greatest percentage of marine life. Other marine fish can be found, but the ling rule.

Ionnis P. Goulandris, courtesy of the U.S. Coast Guard.

IONNIS P. GOULANDRIS

BUILT: 1910
VESSEL TYPE: FREIGHTER
LENGTH: 362 FEET

LOST: DECEMBER 1, 1942
DEPTH: 200 FEET
LOCATION: 26853.9/43577.0

The Ionnis P. Goulandris, a 3,750 ton Greek freighter, in a convoy from Virginia to Maine with a cargo of coal, collided with the Panamanian steamship, Intrepido, approximately 11 miles east of Asbury Park, New Jersey. The Goulandris, nicknamed the "Junior," was rapidly taking on water and radioed for assistance while the crew abandoned ship.

For years there was much speculation on the exact location of the "Junior" and many divers claimed to have dove the wreck. No one, however, was absolutely certain. It was not until the winter of 1973 that the Goulandris' secret hiding place was finally revealed. A team of divers brought up the helm that clearly identified the vessel.

Today, divers enjoy the wreck where she rests in 200 feet of water, 11 miles offshore at the north end of the Mud Hole. The wreckage rises 50 feet off the bottom and is mostly intact. Due to the depth of the site, it is not visited frequently and the dive should only be made by experienced deep divers. Artifacts are easily recovered, and large schools of cod and pollock as well as many lobster inhabit the wreck.

The Jacob M. Haskell is a prime area for shark fishermen during the mako season. This nice mako was taken from the Haskell. Photo by Captain Paul Regula.

JACOB M. HASKELL

BUILT: 1901
VESSEL TYPE: FOUR MASTED
  SCHOONER
LENGTH: 226 FEET

LOST: JUNE 2, 1918
DEPTH: 200 FEET
LOCATION: 26458.1/43165.8

The Jacob M. Haskell was another casualty of "Black Sunday," June 2, 1918. It was noon on that day and all hands but one were below deck eating. A loud explosion echoed from above the four masted schooner and the crew scrambled topside to see what was taking place. Captain William H. Davis sighted the U-boat in the distance, approaching quickly.

When it reached the Haskell, an officer from the submarine and several armed men came aboard and told everyone to abandon the doomed vessel. As the crew gathered together a few cans of water and some biscuits, bombs were placed on the ship. Shortly after, while rowing toward the Jersey coast, they watched in horror as their vessel blew up and slipped beneath the waves.

The remains of the 226 foot Jacob M. Haskell lie 50 miles off Barnegat Inlet. Although the depth of the water is 200 feet, the wreck can be reached at 140 feet. The contents of the cargo has never been disclosed, however, divers have recovered items such as brass bottons, lamps, ironware and more . The area surrounding the Haskell is well known to the tuna and shark fisherman.

USS Jacob Jones, courtesy of the U.S. Navy.

USS JACOB JONES

BUILT: 1918
VESSEL TYPE: NAVY
   DESTROYER
LENGTH: 314 FEET
LOST: FEBRUARY 28, 1942

DEPTH: 115 FEET
LOCATION:
   BOW: 26930.4/42564.5
   BRIDGE: 26929.7/42573.8
   STERN: 26895.1/42544.4

Early in the morning of February 28, 1942, DD130, the USS Jacob Jones, DD130, was torpedoed while cruising the coast, south of Cape May, New Jersey. Only eleven men survived the attack; one hundred and thirty died.

Information about the Jones was gathered primarily from sirvivors' testimony printed in the New York Times and from statements of Captain E.A. Rehwinkel, skipper of the U-578, the submarine that sank the destroyer.

According to Captain E.A. Rehwinkel: "We were ready for action on a predawn patrol when I sighted a ship with no lights, running hard to the starboard. I could not tell what it was, for all I saw in the haze was a silhouette, perhaps a cruiser, I guessed. Torpedoes one, three and five were cleared and we maneuvered to the fore of the vessel to initiate our attack topside. We surfaced and I planned an immediate strike so that we could disperse into deep water before dawn. We moved in so close we were surprised they did not see us. Still we could not determine what kind of ship it was because of the haziness.

"We fired two torpedoes three meters deep and continued moving toward the vessel. I saw four smokestacks and determined that it might be a destroyer. We were so close we had no more time to determine what it was before the first torpedo struck. The direct hit aft of the bridge created a strong explosion and heavy black smoke darkened the sky. The second torpedo struck below the after deck and was followed by a series of loud detonations so violent that we temporarily lost our own electricity. Still running topside, we cruised past the sinking vessel, through the thick black smoke, and returned to the open sea."

The following excerpts from the New York Times are based on survivors' testimony:

"The first torpedo struck the Jacob Jones bow at 4:55 a.m., wrecking the bridge and forward living areas, killing the captain and many of her executive officers. The second torpedo struck the stern, wrecking that section and exploding some of the depth charges. Just about all the survivors were from the midsection which stayed floating for almost an hour, allowing the few men alive to don extra heavy underwear and drink hot coffee.

"Joseph P. Tidwell was the only survivor to say he actually saw the submarine outlined in the morning darkness one hundred yards off the port side. He had just gone to the galley to get sugar for his coffee when the explosion stopped the destroyer dead in the water. Then there was a second explosion, without hesitation Tidwell jumped in the water and climbed into a life raft with two other crew members.

Lobsters are not usually this cooperative, but this one posed long enough for a photo. Photo by Herb Segars.

"Thomas Moody had been in the engine room when the first torpedo hit. He grabbed his coat and a life jacket and rushed topside. He attempted to lower a lifeboat, but the launching equipment was damaged in the explosion and would not operate. After giving up the effort, Moody went below to the storage locker and put on numerous pairs of long underwear and warmed up with coffee. Because the Jacob Jones was sinking fast, Moody jumped into the frigid sea and swam to a life raft. As he got hold of the raft a violent explosion went off as the ship went below the surface."

Today the scattered wreckage of destroyer DD130 lies 30 miles southeast of Cape May, New Jersey. Three main pieces of the Jacob Jones remain with additional debris scattered over a large area. The wreck lies in 115 feet of water rising 15 to 25 feet off the bottom at various points.

From an angling perspective, there are often schools of bluefish cruising the wreck in season, looking for a easy meal. Tiger and brown sharks set up seasonal residence in the wreckage. Blackfish and seabass are in large numbers and divers often must push them aside in search of lobster or artifacts.

For the diver, the Jacob Jones has a lot to offer. However, be sure to heed this. "Don't handle any of the ordinance you will most likely encounter." Although it may no longer be explosive, why risk the chance? Many artifacts are recovered from the wreckage making it one of the better artifact dives in south Jersey. Lobster divers and spear fishermen also enjoy the wreck as they often ascend from the bottom successful in their endeavors.

JOHN MINTURN

BUILT: UNKNOWN
VESSEL TYPE: PASSENGER
  SHIP
LENGTH: UNKNOWN

LOST: FEBRUARY 13, 1846
DEPTH: 0 TO 20 FEET
LOCATION: MANTOLOKING

The square rigged vessel, John Minturn, was lost in a storm considered to be one of the worst of its time. A northeast gale had been blowing since midnight and winds were increasing by the hour. At 9:30 a.m. the John Minturn struck a sandbar 200 yards offshore of Mantoloking. Very little could be done to rescue the 51 trapped passengers and crewmen as the violent sea held them captive. All hopes of a rescue seemed bleak with the rising seas and a heavy snowfall hampering all efforts.

District wreck master, Hugh Johnson, could only wait and pray that the seas would be calm enough for his crew to safely launch a rescue boat to the doomed ship. But by 10 o'clock that evening, cries were heard as the John Minturn broke apart and sank. A few survivors were picked from the ocean, but most fell victim to what was later termed the Minturn storm. On this unforgettable day, February 13, 1846, at least eight other vessels met their fate at the hands of the sea in the trecherous storm.

Located just beyond the surf off Mantoloking, New Jersey, is the scattered wreckage of what is believed to be the John Minturn. The remains of this wooden vessel lie in 20 feet of water and prove to be an interesting dive. Fishermen find fluke, seabass and, in cooler months, ling.

KING COBRA

BUILT: UNKNOWN   **LOST:** FEBRUARY 1979
VESSEL TYPE: TUG BOAT   **DEPTH:** 42 FEET
LENGTH: 82 FEET   **LOCATION:** 27096.1/42675.3

The King Cobra enroute from Greenwich, Connecticut to Camden, New Jersey succumbed to a violent storm south of Cape May. The last radio contact made with the tug boat was off the coast of Atlantic City. All four crew members of the tug were lost when the vessel sank.

In 1981 diver Joe Milligan and a group of fellow divers made the first dive on the tug. A fisherman whose net snagged the wreck shared his loran coordinates with Captain Don Cramer, owner and operator of the fishing/dive vessel Captain Cramers out of Stone Harbor. The divers recovered the tug's binnacle, air horn, two search lights, two portholes and twelve cage lamps. Also recovered was an American flag that was still attached to the mast.

Today, the wreck of the King Cobra is located in 42 feet of water, five miles south of Cape May. The tug is mostly intact and upright with a slight port list. She rises to within 22 feet of the surface. The King Cobra is an excellent second dive of the day. Although few additional artifacts have been recovered from the wreck since that first dive it is certainly worth a try.

Lana Carol, photo by Al Hoffman.

Lana Carol, underwater drawing by Al Hoffman.

LANA CAROL

BUILT: 1973
VESSEL TYPE: FISHING BOAT
LENGTH: 71 FEET

LOST: OCTOBER 31, 1976
DEPTH: 85 FEET
LOCATION: 26859.9/43419.7

For reasons unknown, there is very little information concerning the demise of the Lana Carol and neither local newspapers nor government agencies posses any historical data regarding the demise of this vessel.

Because the wreck of the Lana Carol was such a recent tragedy, the remains are in very good condition. Approximately seven miles southeast of the Manasquan Inlet, the fully intact scallop dredger sits upright in the sand, 85 feet below the surface. Most of her cargo, consisting mainly of scallop shells, remains in the hold of the vessel. Although there is no physical evidence pointing to the cause of why the Lana Carol sank, it is very possible that she encountered heavy seas, capsized and was sent to her sandy grave with all her crew. It has been rumored that the captain purposely overloaded his vessel with scallops, hoping that she would sink so that he could collect the insurance money. This theory has never been proven.

Diving this wreck is very relaxing. It sits upright as if ready to sail. Because she is fully intact you can always find your way back to the anchor, this makes it nice for a night dive. There never appears to be many fish on the wreck, possibly because there are very few crevices for fish to hide.

Lemuel Burrows, courtesy of the U.S. Coast Guard.

LEMUEL BURROWS

BUILT: 1917
VESSEL TYPE: FREIGHTER
LENGTH: 437 FEET

LOST: MARCH 14, 1942
DEPTH: 80 FEET
LOCATION: 26928.2/42991.1

The Lemuel Burrows was on a voyage from Norfolk, Virginia to New York with a full load when she became a victim of the war. The ship, commanded by Captain Clark, was on a northern course following the coast line off Atlantic City, and was proceeding with neither navigational lights nor use of the radio on account of the "black out" regulations imposed by the government during World War II. Without warning a torpedo from a German submarine, the U-404, struck the vessel between the #2 and #3 holds on the starboard side. A few minutes later a second torpedo hit the doomed vessel amidship on the port.

As the crewmen abandoned ship, a third torpedo struck the vessel, lifting the ship and lifeboats in the explosion. She sank quickly to her grave. Lifeboats were upset, drowning their occupants. Of the thirty-four crewmen aboard, only fourteen lived to tell of their horrifying ordeal.

The Lemuel Burrows, built in 1917, measured 437 feet in length and was constructed at the Camden Ship Yard in New Jersey. The vessel was owned by the Mystic Steamship Company.

Today, the remains of the vessel lie scattered on the bottom in 90 feet of water, six miles off the Atlantic City coast. She was dynamited for safe navigational access causing the wreckage to appear now as a mass of twisted steel beams and plates. Over the years the site has been popular with both divers and fishermen.

Lillian, photo by Joe Milligan.

LILLIAN

BUILT: 1920   **LOST:** FEBRUARY 26, 1939
VESSEL TYPE: FREIGHTER   **DEPTH:** 150 FEET
LENGTH: 328 FEET   **LOCATION:** 26697.0/43419.4

On the fog shrouded evening of February 26, 1939, the American Bull Line freighter, Lillian, met her fate when the German freighter, Wiegand, emerged from the fog only 100 yards away. When the Lillian's skipper, Captain Frank Boyer, saw the lights of the approaching ship loom from the heavy mist, he put his ship's wheel hard over and full astern. Captain Leopold Ranitz, master of the Wiegand, ordered his vessel full speed ahead in an attempt to swing away from the impending collision. The 328 foot long Lillian, weighed down with a cargo of sugar, was unable to steer clear of the bow of the Wiegand and she struck the German freighter with such force on the starboard side that it drove the steel plates of the vessel clear out the portside. The Wiegard suffered a 12 foot gash above the water level in the bow, but even worse, the Lillian's bow had been completely severed.

In danger of sinking fast, Captain Boyer ordered his ship abandoned. All 36 crewmen took to the two lifeboats and rowed to safety. The ill-fated freighter slipped beneath the surface southeast of Manasquan Inlet. She's located 17 miles north of where the bow section rests at the site of the collision.

After a Coast Guard investigation into the accident, it was ruled that the captains involved were both guilty of negligently handling their vessels at a speed excessive for the weather conditions.

Today the main hull section of the Lillian lies 26 miles southeast of Manasquan Inlet. She remains upright in 144 feet of water and rises to 105 feet of the surface. The steel skeleton has proven to be an excellent deep water dive site. Many large lobster have been taken from their habitat and many prized artifacts have been recovered.

Fishing over and around the wreckage has been equally rewarding. The area attracts sharks and tuna in season, and year-round maintains a vast array of bottom dwellers.

Lizzie D, photo by John Raguso.

LIZZIE D

BUILT: 1907
VESSEL TYPE: TUG
LENGTH: 77 FEET

LOST: OCTOBER 19, 1922
DEPTH: 80 FEET
LOCATION: 26829.0/43696.3

Although the Lizzie D is just an ordinary tugboat to most people, it was recently discovered that she had an interesting past. Built in 1907, the 77 foot tugboat weighed 122 gross tons and was valued at $25,000. According to the owners, the vessel was cruising the narrows near Sandy Hook when she sank in calm waters. She was carrying no cargo but had eight crew members aboard, all of whom were lost at sea.

Rumors at the time disclosed that the tug was operated by organized crime who used the boat to transport illegal goods. This was never proven, however, and the exact location of the wreck was a well-kept secret for over fifty years.

In July of 1977, Captain John Larsen of the charter boat, Deep Adventures II, while on a dive charter, detected something new on his side scanner. Thinking it could only be the scattered remains of a vessel blanketed with growth, Captain Larsen choose to take a chance and see if his assumptions were correct. Afterwards he was quoted as saying that , "The visibility was super. When I descended down the line and came within sight of the wreck, it was an unbelievable feeling. There was no monofilament on the wreck. Portholes were all over. Lights, ship's bell, everything was still there, however the vessel was deteriorating. I went into its hold and there were bottles of booze all over; thousands of bottles of scotch, bourbon and rum. I didn't recognize any labels, but the whiskey tested alright."

Today the deteriorating remains of the Lizzie D do not resemble those that Captain Larsen remembers, yet it is still an excellent dive site. The wreck lies in 80 feet of water, 19 miles northeast of Shark River Inlet. The pilot house, probably torn off by a dragger, is no longer there. She sits upright, hull intact, with the deck rotting away, making for easy penetration. On occasion, a diver who is willing to dig deeply through the silt in the cargo hold may recover a bottle of booze, sometimes still full.

LIZZIE H. BRAYTON

BUILT: 1891
VESSEL TYPE: FOUR MASTED
  SCHOONER
LENGTH: 201 FEET

LOST: DECEMBER 18, 1904
DEPTH: 10 to 15 FEET
LOCATION: OFF THE BEACH
  AT POINT PLEASANT

An article taken from the "New Jersey Courier" at the time of the wrecking of the Lizzie H. Brayton reports on the demise of this four masted schooner.

"The Brayton struck on the beach at 2 o'clock in the morning. A heavy snow had been falling, but the moonlight made the night unusually light. Just how the Brayton ever got on the beach is a mystery, but it is supposed that her lookout was deceived by the moonlight, and did not see the Sea Girt light because of the falling snow. She was headed northwest when she struck, and came ashore off Point Pleasant.

"Captain Pearce and crew of Bay Head station were soon there, but as there was but little sea, and the vessel and crew were in no danger, they stood by till after daylight, before rigging the breeches buoy. Then the crew of nine men were brought ashore, none the worse from their mishap, except they were pretty well drenched.

"The Brayton was coal laden from Lamberts Point, Virginia, for New Haven, Connecticut. Her only apparent injury Sunday was to her rudder, which was disabled. The weather was mild, there was no wind and little surf.

"C. Kelly has sailed for twenty-eight years and this was the first mishap at sea he had ever had. She was built in 1891 at Bath, Maine, and is 201 feet long. Her net tonnage is 979 tons.

"Unfortunately a few days later a northeastern struck the coast and swamped the Lizzie H. Brayton. She sank to the bottom. All that was left above the water line was salvaged after the storm abated but most was left to the sea."

Divers Carlos Narciso, Tom Nolan and Howard Rothweiler first dove the wreck in February 1990. During a visit to the Brielle Dive Shop, owner Bill Schmoldt told them of a wreck he had snorkeled as a child. One blustery winter day after receiving the location and ranges of the wreck, the three divers swam out toward the Brayton.

When arriving at the site they noticed a slight disturbance on the surface of the water in the vicinity of where the wreck was suppose to be.

According to diver Howard Rothweiler, "Within five minutes we were suited up and swimming out to the wreck. Sure enough when we dove near the disturbance we landed right on the wreck. The wreck was made up of wood with lots of brass spikes holding it together. Unexpectedly it was still fairly intact, considering that it was an old wooden wreck that had been beaten by the waves over the past 86 years. The wreck sticks up about five feet from the bottom and the inshore side is slightly washed out. The best artifacts we managed to find were lots of umbrella rigs that fishermen had snagged on the wreck while trolling close to shore."

Howard noted that on their dive, marine life was nearly nonexistent. This can be partially accounted for by the winter season in which the dive occurred.

The wreck of the Lizzie H. Brayton is located 160 yards off the beach in Point Pleasant. The wreckage lies north to south in 10 -15 feet of water and is best visited at high tide. By using the southern section of the Driftwood motel as a land range and swimming directly east, you can't miss the wreck. As with all beach dives, diver etiquette should be followed. Be sure to obtain permission when accessing private property and don't leave behind garbage. Follow the rules of the community.

LOGWOOD WRECK

VESSEL TYPE: SCHOONER
DEPTH: 90 FEET
CONSTRUCTION: WOOD
LOCATION: 26856.4/43474.6

An unidentified wreck nine miles east of the Manasquan Inlet is that of a schooner barge laden with large boulders. It is believed that the barge was in tow northbound, because of the direction in which the bow is now resting on the bottom. The cargo of large boulders were possibly to be used in bridge or jetty construction. Over the years the wreck has broken open with much of her cargo outlining the shape of the vessel. The barge has a profile of being just over two hundred feet long and fifty feet wide. She rises only five feet off the bottom with deep holes burrowed into the sand.

Blackfish are abundant on the wreck, with many of them exceeding five pounds. While making a surface interval, inbetween dives, divers often spend their time fishing and fill coolers full of these big, tasty fish.

Diving the Logwood is worth the trip. Visibility is generally good, often over thirty feet. Lobstering requires a lobster hook if you plan to capture the "giant bugs," due to the deep recesses under the wood. Even then, the ten pounders are often out of reach. Spearfishing, photography or sightseeing are always enjoyable. To date no artifacts have been recovered which might help identify the vessel.

MALTA

BUILT: UNKNOWN
VESSEL TYPE: STEAMSHIP
LENGTH: UNKNOWN

LOST: DECEMBER 11, 1885
DEPTH: 15 FEET
LOCATION: BELMAR,

The steamship Malta, a vessel of 1,000 gross ton registry, came ashore at 3:30 a.m. off Belmar, New Jersey. The ship struck head on and, assisted by the pounding sea, slowly turned broadside.

Two minutes after running aground, the surfmen from the nearby Life Saving Station came to the rescue and attempted to shoot a rescue line across the bow of the stricken vessel. On the third try, the crew aboard the Malta caught the line and secured it twenty feet up the foremast. Thirty-three crew members were safely brought ashore and only one life was lost. A sailor panicked, jumped overboard, and tried to swim ashore but drowned.

After numerous futile attempts to free the ship, the cargo, consisting of 10,000 barrels of oil, was removed. Finally, on December 11, 1885, the Malta surrendered to the sea and broke amidship. She was considered a total loss.

On Christmas day, a derelict barge was sent by a wrecking company to try and salvage the remains of the Malta, but due to heavy seas and a rough surf, the barge abandoned its mission and returned to New York.

Today, the wreckage of the steamer lies one hundred yards off the beach in Belmar. Because the remains of the Malta are close to the Shark River Inlet, visibility is sometimes reduced to nothing, and there are occasions when the wreck is completely covered by sand. Many artifacts have been recovered from the Malta and an anchor can still be seen rising from the silt. Normally only small fish inhabit the area, most of them bergall.

MANASQUAN WRECK

VESSEL TYPE: SAILING SHIP
DEPTH: 20 FEET
CONSTRUCTION: WOOD/METAL
LOCATION: 26945.2/43497.3

The true identity of the Manasquan Wreck is one of the many mysteries of the sea. Diver Howard Rothwieler, who has made many dives on this wreck, is in constant pursuit of its actual name. Howard describes the site as "Very interesting if you can put up with poor visibility and mild current from the Manasquan Inlet." The remains are approximately 80 feet long, 20 feet wide, and at the highest point rise only five feet off the bottom. Howard indicated that "A majority of the wreck is made up of wooden planking held together with brass spikes, and covered in areas with copper sheeting. The entire wreck is overgrown with a light marine growth. Around the site are ballast stones, wooden debris and large barrels containing cargo."

Located one-quarter of a mile north of the inlet and an equal distance from the shore, this dive site is accessible from the beach. It is suggested, however, that if you are not a top notch swimmer, a boat is the safest way to visit the wreck.

During the past year, Rothwieler and fellow divers, Tom Nolan and Carlos Narciso, have recovered many artifacts from the wreck. These include various style knives with wooden handles, chains, files, flat irons, draw knives with ornate brass tips, candlestick holders, hinge-style folding eyeglasses, brass and steel padlocks, flint, clock parts, various styles of buttons, china, pen knives, brass straight pins and liquor barrel taps. Most of the artifacts recovered were contained in wooden barrels which required the diver to break them open. Some of the barrels were broken open by storms and their contents are now buried in the sand around the wreck.

A very interesting marine population inhabits the wreck. In the winter months a resident seal makes the site its hunting ground, feeding on shrimp, mussels and sea anemones. In early spring as the water begins to warm, winter flounder and ling are found in large quantities. The summer months bring the largest concentration of fish to the wreck site. Blackfish, seabass, porgies, sea robbins, fluke, bluefish and large schools of bait fish roam the remains. Howard speared a seven and a half pound blackfish on one dive

This was a lucky find. Tom Nolan and Carlos Narciso recovered the rudder post from the Manasquan Wreck.

and noted many more that were larger.

Just east of the Manasquan Wreck where the water depth drops to thirty feet, fluke are found on the hard mud bottom. Howard commented that there are not only a lot of fluke, but many large fish that weigh over five pounds. The largest fluke that he has speared near the wreck was twelve pounds.

Diver Howard Rothweiler speared this 12 pound fluke while diving on the Manasquan Wreck. Photo by Dolores Rothweiler.

MARYLAND

BUILT: 1891
VESSEL TYPE: BARGE
LENGTH: 236 FEET

LOST: DECEMBER 4, 1911
DEPTH: 25 FEET
LOCATION: LUDLAM BEACH,
SEA ISLE CITY

The barge, Maryland, was being towed north to New York with a load of coke when she foundered just off the beach at Sea Isle City. Her tow tug cut her free and she drifted inshore and sank in 25 feet of water. Her sinking is not as exciting as her past.

When built in 1891 she was christened as the General Slocum, a paddle wheel vessel used on the Hudson River where she transported tourists. On the morning of June 15, 1904, her three decks were overloaded with 1,500 passengers.

Shortly after disembarking, a fire broke out below decks and quickly spread through the three decks of the General Slocum. Her wooden super structure quickly ignited, forcing passengers to jump into the water. Many passengers not knowing how to swim, huddled together on the decks and prayed.

The General Slocum continued to burn right down to the water line. When the disaster was finally over, officials estimated as many as 1,200 passengers lost their lives.

In 1907 the burned-out hull was purchased and converted into a barge and was renamed the Maryland. In 1909 the barge was loaded with a cargo of 500,000 bricks and sank at the dock when the tide dropped. Her seam split and she had to be off-loaded and repaired.

After repairs, the Maryland was back in service being towed up and down the coast until December 4, 1911, when she finally wrecked off Sea Isle City.

Today, the remains of the barge are reported in two different locations. One report lists the Maryland as being 20 miles off Atlantic City in 180 feet of water. This wreck site I'm not familiar with. The Maryland I know is located 300 yards off the northern section beach at Sea Isle City. Most of the wreckage is covered over by the sand, but with changing currents and storms, often the wreck is exposed.

127

Maurice Tracy, courtesy of the U.S. Coast Guard.

MAURICE TRACY

BUILT: 1916
VESSEL TYPE: COLLIER
LENGTH: 253 FEET

LOST: JUNE 17, 1944
DEPTH: 70 FEET
LOCATION: 26889.8/43356.9

The collier, Maurice Tracy, registered at 1,509 gross tons, was built in 1916 by the Great Lake Engine Works Company and owned by M. & J. Tracy, Inc. She was struck broadside at 3:45 a.m. by an unidentified liberty ship. The Tracy, listing severely and in danger of sinking was abandoned by her crew. Minutes later, the 253 foot ship sank below the surface narrowly sparing the lives of those on board.

The wreckage now lies five miles east of Seaside Heights, New Jersey in 80 feet of water. Because the ship was a navigational hazard, the vessel was leveled by dynamite so that the remains now rise to 60 feet of the surface. This wreck usually proves to be an interesting one with an abundance of sea life including a large variety of bottom fish, crabs and lobster. Artifacts are occasionally recovered by a lucky diver.

Mohawk, photo by Mike Sonta.

MOHAWK

BUILT: 1926
VESSEL TYPE: PASSENGER
  LINER
LENGTH: 387 FEET

LOST: JANUARY 25, 1935
DEPTH: 80 FEET
LOCATION: 26878.0/43439.9

In a dense fog during the year 1929, the Clyde Line steamer, Mohawk, left New York Harbor on an eight day cruise. Three miles off the Atlantic Highlands she collided with the Old Dominion steamer, Jefferson. Realizing that the liner was badly damaged and in danger of sinking, the captain purposely ran his ship aground. No one was injured. The ship was towed to the shipyard for repair work and did not return to service until the fall of 1931.

The Mohawk was then commanded by Captain Joseph E. Wood and carried miscellaneous cargo which included U.S. Army jeep parts, lumber, tile and machinery. The 387 foot vessel left the East River pier bound for Havana and Vera Cruz at 4:00 p.m. on January 25, 1935. She passed Sandy Hook at 5:30 p.m. A much slower Norwegian freighter, the Talisman, left the 30th Street Pier in Brooklyn at 5:00 p.m. and did not pass Sandy Hook until 7:06 p.m. She was enroute to Clairmont, Delaware to be loaded with additional cargo bound for Brazil.

How the Mohawk sank on that night is no mystery, but the circumstances that lead up to the sinking have never been explained. She was the faster of the two vessels and had passed Sandy Hook almost an hour and a half ahead of the freighter. This made officials believe that the Mohawk should have been approximately 25 miles ahead of the Talisman, but this was not so. Nine o'clock that evening, the 25th, eight miles off Sea Girt, New Jersey, the freighter tore a hole in the Mohawk's side. Captain Wood first attempted to beach the vessel, but the entire room flooded. She listed and sank in less than an hour. Due to the severe list of the ship and the icy condition of the lifeboats, only a few were lowered. Four lifeboats with 97 survivors were picked up by a passing ship. Unfortunately, 45 others lost their lives.

After questioning passengers and crew, officials discerned that it was possible the Mohawk's steering had either frozen or that the cables attached to the rudder had broken, forcing the ship to travel in a large circle. This would have given the Talisman time to catch up

131

**Everything from school pollock to huge blackfish can be found on the Mohawk.
Photo by Pete Barrett.**

to the faster moving Mohawk. Although no definite cause was ever given, this reasoning seems most plausible. The wreck lies beneath 80 feet of water, eight miles east of the Manasquan Inlet.

From 1935 until the ship was cleared in 1942, the Mohawk rose to within 30 feet of the surface. It was not until a Coast Guard cutter tracked a German U-boat to its hiding place, the Mohawk, that it was deemed necessary to demolish the sunken vessel. The wreckage now rises only 20 feet from the bottom and resembles a scrap yard. Large lobster inhabit the wreck as well as many different species of fish. In the spring, ling run over the site, you have to beat them away to see the wreckage. Artifacts such as flatware, plates, tile and nautical hardware are often recovered.

Northern Pacific

NORTHERN PACIFIC

BUILT: 1915
VESSEL TYPE: PASSENGER
   LINER
LENGTH: 525 FEET

LOST: FEBRUARY 8, 1922
DEPTH: 145 FEET
LOCATION: 26896.9/42558.9

The Northern Pacific was built in Philadelphia, Pennsylvania by William Cramp & Sons Ship & Engine Building for the Great Northern Pacific Steamship Company. She was a massive vessel for that time period with a length of 525 feet, a beam of 63 feet and a depth of 21 feet. Her gross tonnage was 8,255.

Put into service on the West Coast she carried 550 first class passengers, 108 second class, 198 third and maintained a crew of 224. Until late 1917 she ran a variety of West Coast services including a cruise from San Francisco to Honolulu.

In late 1917, the Northern Pacific was acquired by the United States Navy and refitted for military service as a Navy transport. She operated between New Jersey and France carrying troops and wounded back home.

In August 1919, she was decommissioned and plans were made to refurbish her into a passenger liner once again.

On February 8, 1922 she was sailing 25 miles southeast of Cape May with 74 people aboard. At 12:55 a.m. a fire was discovered, which quickly enveloped the ship. Everyone aboard, but four, were able to abandon ship and were spared their lives. The fire raged out of control until the Northern Pacific finally rolled over and sank.

Her remains lie upside down in 145 feet of water. She rises 25 feet off the ocean floor and intact. Visibility is generally good, often more than fifty feet. During the warmer months anglers report catching tuna, marlin and sharks around the site. Diver Joe Milligan noted that because the north side of the wreck is washed out, the south side is the place to hunt for artifacts.

NORTHWEST BARGES

VESSEL TYPE: BARGE
DEPTH: 60 FEET
CONSTRUCTION: WOOD
LOCATION: 26878.9/43295.3

In sixty feet of water, four miles northeast of the Barnegat Inlet are the remains of the Northwest Barges. The origin of the nickname given to this site is unknown to modern day divers and fishermen. Some speculate the name was given as a reference to its location from the Barnegat Lightship.

The wreckage is best known as a fishing spot. In the summer season porgies make the area their home and are in abundance. Black seabass, ling, cunner, bergall, tog, eel pout and monkfish are also often caught. In and around the sand, fluke are taken by those using live killies.

The low profile of the wreck and its close proximity to the shore deter most divers. Her wooden ribbing gives the appearance of a grid pattern on the ocean floor. The remains are scattered over a large area and those who dive here are often in search of lobster. The lobster taken from the Northwest Barges vary in size and are usually of the smaller variety. Visibility is often poor, averaging less than ten feet. Nevertheless the site is a good one for novice divers because there is little danger of getting tangled in the wreck and the depth is shallow.

OKLAHOMA

BUILT: 1908
VESSEL TYPE: TANKER
LENGTH: 419 FEET

LOST: JANUARY 4, 1914
DEPTH: 80 FEET
LOCATION: BOW 26972.4/42277.2
STERN: 26717.9/43079.4

During the morning of January 4, 1914, the tanker, Oklahoma, was bound for Boston from Philadelphia when she experienced gale force winds and heavy seas. Captain Gunther, knowing his journey would last just one day and that his ship was only seven years old, saw no danger in sight.

Twelve hours out of port and seven miles off Block Island, the Oklahoma, according to a report by Captain Gunther, was picked up by two giant waves; one on the bow and one on the stern. They suspended the ship out of the water and, without warning, the tanker split in two.

The stern section of the Oklahoma sank in the high seas. The men adrift on the bow seemed doomed as well. There were numerous attempts by passing ships to lower lifeboats, only to have them crash against their own vessel or be swallowed by the sea. It appeared hopeless as the bow section continued to float south. After almost 24 hours, the seas calmed enough so that the revenue cutter Seneca was able to dispatch a rescue crew of eight volunteers to remove the survivors. All were injured or near death due to the cold.

The bow section was taken in tow by the Seneca and brought to a shipyard in Bayonne, New Jersey where it was cut up for scrap. The stern section drifted for almost ten days below the surface, undetected until it was spotted approximately eight miles off Seaside Heights, New Jersey. The Seneca once again was summoned to the drifting wreckage to sink her. After making a search of the vessel and recovering three bodies, 15 shots had to be torn into her before she settled to the bottom.

To date, the exact location of the Oklahoma is not known. Many wrecks, however, are located in the area where the Coast Guard reported the sinking. These include the Emerald Wreck, the Coin Wreck, and a few other small pieces. It is possible that these are parts of the Oklahoma. It is also possible that the Oklahoma is still drifting below the surface. This is not inconceivable since one

Oklahoma, courtesy of The Steamship Historical Society, University of Baltimore Library.

derelict was reported to have floated from Greenland to Florida and then back north again. Another derelict was spotted on numerous occasions during a forty year period before she was finally laid to rest. The Oklahoma joins these ships, and many others, as yet another unsolved mystery of the sea.

ONE TWENTY WRECK

VESSEL TYPE: STEAMSHIP
DEPTH: 80 FEET
CONSTRUCTION: WOOD/STEEL
LOCATION: 26873.4/43468.3

The shipwreck known as the One Twenty Wreck was given its name because of the compass heading used from the Manasquan Inlet to reach the site.

The remains appear to be that of a steamship from the late 1800s. Artifacts recovered from the wreck resemble the style of others recovered from other vessels during that time period. The wreckage is widely scattered over a large area. Both wooden deck and metal hull material make up the largest sections. Heavy machinery, winches and gears are easily identified in the midsection. The remains of the One twenty Wreck rest in 80 feet of water approximately six miles northeast of Manasquan Inlet.

Numerous artifacts, mostly nautical ones, have been recovered. Lobster is the main attraction of the site and often game bags are brought to the surface full. On one evening dive, diver Bill Ryan and the author captured twenty-four lobster, all extremely large.

A variety of fish can be caught when anchored over the wreck site. These include ling, black seabass, tog, cunner, eel pouts and fluke. Because of the distance between pieces, it may at times, be necessary to take in or put out more anchor line until you hit the right spot on the wreck.

The Oregon sinking to her final resting place.

OREGON

BUILT: 1881
VESSEL TYPE: PASSENGER
   LINER
LENGTH: 518 FEET

LOST: MARCH 14, 1886
DEPTH: 130 FEET
LOCATION: 26453.1/43676.5

Built in Glasgow, Scotland in 1881, the Oregon was a Cunard Line vessel of 7,375 gross tons. She was one of the largest ships in her day with a length of 518 feet, a beam of 54 feet and a hull depth of 40 feet. Her massive engines could produce 13,000 horsepower and consumed almost 250 tons of coal daily to average a cruising speed of eighteen knots.

On her maiden voyage she won a blue ribbon for making the transatlantic crossing from Queenstown to Sandy Hook in less than nine days. In 1884 she broke her own record by making the crossing in less than seven days.

On the early morning of March 14, 1886, just a few hours before she would dock in New York, the Oregon collided with an unidentified schooner five miles off Fire Island, New York. The schooner was believed to have been that of the Charles R. Morse, since she too was reported missing that same day. The schooner slipped beneath the waves and neither she nor her crew were ever seen again.

As the sun rose on the morning of March 14, 1886, it was apparent that the Oregon was not going to stay afloat. Captain Cottier gave the order to lower the lifeboats just as two rescue vessels arrived. The pilot boat, Phantom, was scheduled to pilot the liner to port and with the assistance of the schooner, Fannie A. Gorthan, all 845 passengers and crew of the Oregon were rescued without incident.

She stayed afloat for approximately eight hours then settled below the surface and sank to the bottom. The remains of the liner lie twenty-one miles east of Fire Island in 130 feet of water. It has been suggested by many that this wreck is one of the greatest dives off Long Island. It would be difficult to view the entire wreck during

Nice size blackfish are quite abound on the Oregon. Photo by Captain Paul Regula.

a single dive. She is facing north with her large engine rising ten to twenty feet off the bottom. In front of the engine is a series of boilers which normally are surrounded by school-size cod and pollack. Many artifacts have been recovered and seabass and blackfish abound. In the stern of the wreck more artifacts including plates, cups, flatware have been recovered with the Cunard Steamship Company insignia on them. The sides of the wreck have finally given in to the eroding sea and she now lays open with her engine and boilers exposed. Visibility is virtually always exceptional, averaging thirty feet.

Many divers are attracted to wrecks for the many artifacts that can be found. This lucky diver displays an aluminum soup bowl.

Patrice McAllister, photo by Steve Lang, Tug Boat Photo Research.

PATRICE McALLISTER

BUILT: 1919
VESSEL TYPE: TUG BOAT
LENGTH: 94 FEET

LOST: OCTOBER 4, 1976
DEPTH: 55 FEET
LOCATION: 26930.5/43061.5

The Patrice McAllister, built in 1919 weighed 201 gross tons and her dimensions were 94 feet in length with a 24 foot beam and a hull depth of 12 feet. Owned by McAllister Brothers, Inc. of New York the tug was registered and operated mostly from the port of Philadelphia, Pennsylvania.

Information taken from the Coast Guard inquiry into her sinking on November 29, 1976 gives the following account for the demise of the vessel:

"The Patrice McAllister, a tug normally utilized for protected harbor operations, could not withstand the rigors of being towed at approximately seven knots, in 15-20 knot winds, and four to six foot seas. The investigation was severely limited in that the tug sank during the night without any eyewitnesses, and was subsequently declared a total loss.

"The tug Judith McAllister was towing her sister tug from Camden, New Jersey to Jersey City for major repairs. The tug and crew departed the piers on October 1st. The Patrice was being towed alongside the Judith when their journey began, but when they entered the vicinity of Fourteen Foot Bank in Delaware Bay the Patrice was put on hawser to see how she would follow. After a few adjustments she followed straight and the journey commenced.

"On October 3rd the tug and tow cleared the Delaware Bay entrance into the ocean where the seas were moderate and winds calm.

"On October 4th the skipper of the towing tug reduced speed off Atlantic City due to increasing winds of 15-20 knots and building seas of 4-6 feet. Three miles north of Brigantine Shoals it was observed that the Judith McAllister was no longer moving and that the tow lights on the Patrice McAllister could no longer be seen.

"The skipper of the Judith notified the Coast Guard at daybreak of the sinking and stayed attached to the sunken tug until a Coast Guard buoy was placed over the wreck."

Today, the full intact remains of the sunken tug lie four miles east of Brigantine Inlet in 55 feet of water. There are blankets of mussels covering the wreck and local wreck fish include seabass and blackfish. The wreck sits upright and is easy to penetrate for divers.

Persephone, courtesy of The National Archives.

PERSEPHONE

BUILT: 1925   **LOST:** MAY 25, 1942
VESSEL TYPE: TANKER   **DEPTH:** 55 FEET
LENGTH: 468 FEET   **LOCATION:** 26895.2/43289.5

The year 1942 proved to be a grim one for merchant shipping off the Atlantic coast. The sinking of numerous vessels by the U-boat fleet, including the Gulf Trade, the Maurice Tracy and the R.P. Resor, forced extreme caution be taken by merchant seamen. The most common precaution was to travel in convoys on a zig-zag course.

On May 15th, the Persephone, enroute from Aruba to New York with a cargo of fuel oil, was traveling in a convoy with twenty other ships. Being in the middle of the convoy, Captain Quistagaard felt relatively safe and was not worried that his vessel was unarmed. Ten days out of port, at 2:00 p.m. and only 2.5 miles east of Barnegat Light, a torpedo tore into the engine room and the ship was stopped in the water. Only 45 seconds later another torpedo struck the starboard side at midships and the stern of the Persephone sank to the bottom. Nine seamen were taken with her.

The bow section of the tanker remained above the water until salvage attempts were made and she broke in two. On August 1, 1942, this section was brought to Gravesent Bay, New York where it was beached. Twenty-one thousand barrels of oil were then off-loaded.

The tanker was constructed in 1925 by Fried, Drupp Germainia Weft who, ironically, also built U-boats in Kiel Garden, Germany. The Persephone was 468 feet in length, had a 63 foot beam and a 27 foot draft. She was owned by the Panamanian Transport Company.

Today, the tanker's stern lies in 50 to 60 feet of water. Most of the scattered wreckage is made up of her heavy machinery. Due to its shallow depth, the site is visited often by dive boats from Barnegat bringing students for certification dives. In the summer months there are plenty of fish but very few lobster. When lobster are found they are somewhat larger than usual. A twenty pound lobster captured on the Persephone made quite a tasty meal one summer day for the author.

The sinking of the Persephone was the closest to the shoreline of the Atlantic coast during the Second World War.

Pinta, photo by Joe Paola.

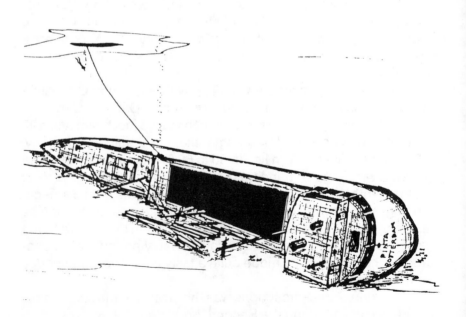

Pinta, underwater drawing by Al Hoffman.

PINTA

BUILT: 1959
VESSEL TYPE: FREIGHTER
LENGTH: 194 FEET

LOST: MAY 7, 1963
DEPTH: 90 FEET
LOCATION: 26880.5/43563.5

The 194 foot Dutch motor ship, Pinta, inbound from Central America to New York with a cargo of lumber, was broadsided a few minutes after sunset by the freighter, City of Perth. The Coast Guard described the weather conditions at the time as clear with visibility of fifteen miles and moderate seas. A southeast wind was blowing at seventeen knots.

At 7:18 p.m. the freighter radioed the Coast Guard that she had struck the Pinta and both vessels were taking on water. A few minutes later, another message from the City of Perth told authorities that the crew of the Dutch ship had abandoned their vessel. At 8:46 p.m. the City of Perth sent one last message stating that no assistance was needed; all crew members of the Pinta had been taken safely aboard. The Pinta herself, however, was badly listing to the port side.

Approximately fifteen minutes later, the crews of the two ships stood on the deck and watched the Dutch ship disappear below the surface. After a Coast Guard inquiry, the decision was made not to remove or blow up the 1,000 gross ton ship because she was not a navigational hazard.

Twenty-seven years later, divers can still see lettering on the stern of the wreck. She rests on the bottom in 90 feet of water, almost six and a half miles off the coast near Shark River Inlet. The Pinta is excellent for the underwater photographer. When fishing this wreck, keep in mind that it is intact and lying on her port side. It is best to fish midships where many of the bottom dwellers hide inside the vessel.

Pliny, photo by Joe Milligan.

PLINY

BUILT: 1878
VESSEL TYPE: PASSENGER
FREIGHTER
LENGTH: 288 FEET

LOST: MAY 13, 1882
DEPTH: 20 FEET
LOCATION: 26949.2/43579.8

The steamship, Pliny, washed ashore at Deal Beach, New Jersey on May 14, 1882. Bound for New York from Rio De Janeiro, the passenger freighter was carrying twenty-one passengers and a large crew.

The cargo consisted of 20,000 bags of coffee and 500 hides, all to be brought to Wall Street for trade. The steamer was owned by Lambert & Holt of Liverpool. Built in Barrow, England in 1878, the Pliny was an iron steamship of 1,069 gross tons, approximately 200 feet in length.

As the stranded vessel laid helpless in the breakers, curious onlookers watched the crew of the ship and workers of Life Saving Station #5 and #6 remove the cargo. The crew's work continued for two days. On the morning of the 16th, the ship broke in two and sank. It was discovered later that a passenger had 3,000 dollars in gold coins locked up in the safe of the captain's cabin. It is assumed that the safe was never recovered.

The remains of the Pliny lie approximately 200 feet off the beach at Deal, New Jersey in 20 feet of water. Fishing the wreck from the beach in the fall has proven very rewarding. Striped bass and bluefish are taken regularly from the wreckage. Diving is interesting because she sits in a hole about five feet below the ocean floor. There are times when this wreck is completely covered by sand.

RC Mohawk, courtesy of the U.S. Navy.

RC MOHAWK

BUILT: 1904
VESSEL TYPE: REVENUE
   CUTTER
LENGTH: 205 FEET

LOST: OCTOBER 1, 1917
DEPTH: 105 FEET
LOCATION: 26867.6/43670.7

The Revenue Cutter, Mohawk, was built in 1904 for the U.S. Treasury Department to assist vessels in need from Delaware Bay north. Built in Richmond, Virginia, she weighed 980 gross tons and her dimensions were 205 feet in length with a 32 foot beam and 11 foot hull depth. For over twelve years the RC Mohawk sailed up and down the East Coast with few unusual occurrences.

During the First World War she was commissioned by the U.S. Navy to help patrol the approaches to New York. On October 1st, while patrolling in the northern Mud Hole, the cutter collided with the British vessel, Vennacher, traveling in a convoy when the RC Mohawk entered into her path. All crew members on board the revenue cutter were spared injury.

Today, the remains of the cutter lie eight miles east of Sandy Hook Bay in 105 feet of water. The stern of the vessel is mostly intact and she is lying on her starboard side. The midsection of the wreck lies open to divers who might want to try exploring her engine room. Unfortunately due to her location in the Mud Hole, visibility is usually poor.

Fishing the midsection of the wreck, or the low spot on your depth recorder, is the best bet. Often large head (monk) fish are caught. Seabass and blackfish inhabit most of the wreckage with the largest concentration at the stern.

Relief Lightship WAL-505, courtesy of the U.S. Coast Guard.

RELIEF LIGHTSHIP WAL-505

BUILT: 1904
VESSEL TYPE: LIGHTSHIP
LENGTH: 129 FEET

LOST: JUNE 24, 1960
DEPTH: 110 FEET
LOCATION: 26903.5/43695.9

The Relief Lightship, WAL-505, with white lettering on a red hull, sank in only ten minutes after being struck by a cargo vessel. The original Ambrose lightship, the WAL-614, had been brought into port for scheduled maintenance work and the WAL-505 put into service to keep the busy shipping traffic in the New York Bight navigable.

It was 4:05 a.m. when the 10,270 gross ton C-2 cargo vessel, Green Bay, struck the lightship just behind midsection at a right angle. Water flooded both the engine and compressor rooms causing the ship to list 15 degrees. The nine Coast Guard members crew aboard the stricken vessel remained calm and, displaying professionalism, followed the procedures for abandoning ship. All escaped without injury.

Navy divers investigated the scene of the disaster the next day and found a 12 foot long gash in the starboard side. It was concluded that the puncture was so large that the crew would not have been able to keep the Relief WAL-505 afloat.

The remains of the 129 foot lightship lie in almost 100 feet of water, miles east of the Sandy Hook. The wreck rises 30 feet from the sand with her two giant mast lying nearby. The arrival of warmer water often attracts porgies and flounder to the wreck site.

REMEDIOS PASCUE ("BONE WRECK")

BUILT: 1885   **LOST:** JANUARY 3, 1903
VESSEL TYPE: STEAMSHIP   **DEPTH:** 20 FEET
LENGTH: 216 FEET   **LOCATION:** 26886.7/43289.7

This three masted Spanish schooner left Buenos Aires on October 18, 1902 destined for New York on what was said to have been an eventful journey. The fully rigged ship, built in 1885 in Barton, Nova Scotia, was registered at 1,605 gross tons. The trip should have taken only 50 days, however, because of alternating light winds and heavy storms, the journey took longer. To add to the misfortune, two crew members died of fever on the way.

It was a foggy night on January 3rd and Captain Tablo Ganto had his ship follow the lights of the shore line. He made the mistake, though, of allowing his vessel to drift too close to shore and it struck a sand bar off Ship Bottom, New Jersey.

Keeper Truex of the #20 Life Saving Station saw the vessel in distress and summoned his crew to the beach to render assistance. Two lines were shot over the ship but the sailors on board were too frightened and did not reel in the breeches buoy. The rescuers then attempted to launch a lifeboat to the ship. This was accomplished. After arguing about who was to be taken off the ship first, four trips were made and all crew members were brought ashore safely.

Following futile attempts to free the Remedios Pascue, the wrecking ship North America came to help salvage some cargo and try to pull the doomed vessel off the bar. Finally the ship's timbers gave in and she broke apart and sank, taking most of the cargo with her to the bottom.

Today, the remains of the "Bone Wreck" lie 200 yards off the beach in Ship Bottom. The depth over the wreck varies between 20 to 30 feet depending on the tide. Much of the vessel's cargo still remains scattered around the site. This includes animal bones and hides, and explains why the wreck was nicknamed the "Bone Wreck." Fishing or diving this site is best done by making the short trip south out of the Barnegat Inlet by boat. Seabass and blackfish can be found on the wreck year-round and occasionally a large lobster is caught by a lucky diver.

RIGGI BARGES

VESSEL TYPE: BARGE(S)
DEPTH: 75 FEET
CONSTRUCTION: WOOD
LOCATION: 26906.6/43449.4

Just inshore of the Manasquan Ridge, five miles southeast of the inlet is a barge wreck known only as the Riggi Barges. Some believe there are three barges located at the wreck site. These are the Valparsio, Hillville and John N. Winstead, that sank around the same time the Riggi Barges were discovered. However, divers who visit the site, often in pursuit of lobster, are skeptical due to the size of the remains. It is certain that the scattered remains are those of at least one barge.

The wreck lies in 75 feet of water and is low to the sand. Most of what is exposed are the wooden ribs and decaying hull. The wrecks rise only five feet off the bottom and, at varying times, more or less of the wreck is exposed. Fishing the area for seabass is very productive with most fish of school size but large in number. Occasionally bluefish are taken. The challenge with blues is to keep them from tangling the fishing line in the wreckage.

RJUKAN

BUILT: UNKNOWN   **LOST:** DECEMBER 26, 1876
VESSEL TYPE: STEAM SHIP   **DEPTH:** 25 FEET
LENGTH: 160 FEET   **LOCATION:** BRADLEY BEACH

In the early morning of December 26th, after taking on a pilot at Staten Island, the captain of the 160 foot Norwegian ship, Rjukan, ventured too close to a sand bar. Realizing the strong winds from the northeast would be trying to take the vessel ashore, he attempted to turn and pull away from land. Before she could be moved a safe distance from shore, the strong winds picked her up and carried her aground.

At 6:30 a.m., a beachcomber noticed the stranded vessel and called for assistance. The Life Saving crew arrived at the scene with all their equipment except the most important; the lifeboat. A local sea captain seeing the confusion launched his own boat and by making several trips, rescued all twenty crew members of the Rjukan within hours. By nightfall, the vessel had been broken apart by the heavy surf and laid to rest on the bottom.

Today the scattered wreckage of the Rjukan lies 200 feet off the beach in 25 feet of water. The wreck is found outside the surf at Bradley Beach. Many relics from the late 1800s have been recovered and include pottery, coins, brass and nautical hardware.

R.P. RESOR

BUILT: 1936
VESSEL TYPE: TANKER
LENGTH: 435 FEET

LOST: FEBRUARY 28, 1942
DEPTH: 130 FEET
LOCATION: 26638.3/43277.1

Unlike most ships, the R.P. Resor became famous while being built. In 1935, the Federal Shipbuilding and Dry Dock Company of Kearny, New Jersey realized the demand for a new type of construction to take the place of the old style tankers. They designed a new class of tanker and installed more efficient and more economical equipment to compliment the new breed of vessel. The R.P. Resor was the most modern oil carrier of her size and construction in the world. She was a single screw ship of 12,875 deadweight tons, had a draft of 28 feet and an overall length of 435 feet. Her cargo capacity was 105,025 barrels of oil. When fully loaded her certified speed was 12.7 knots.

Due to numerous reports of submarine sightings up and down the East Coast, the captain of the R.P. Resor gave the command to steer in zig-zag course. This was to be done from Miami to New Jersey. A lookout and armed guards were posted on the ship in an effort to detect and fend off any U-boats encountered.

On the evening of February 26th, Captain Marcus was at the helm and reported in his log that the night was fine and clear with a light northwesterly breeze. There was a small ripple on the water and the passage was lit by the moonlight. At 8:00 p.m. that evening, Captain Marcus stepped off the bridge when he was relieved by Able Seaman, John Forsdal. Approximately two hours later, some 20 miles east of Manasquan Inlet, Navy gunners mate, Daniel Huey, reported seeing lights off the Resor's port bow. Forsdal also saw the lights but because they were so dim he could not determine the ship's size. The mysterious vessel then turned off its lights and disappeared into the darkness.

A few minutes later there was a violent explosion on the port side. In what seemed only seconds, the R.P. Resor was aflame from her bridge aft. Forsdal, getting back on his feet after being knocked to the deck, realized that he and gunners mate, Daniel Huey, were cut off from the rest of the crew. They quickly lowered a lifeboat and rowed 100 yards clear of the burning ship. From there they saw the silhouette of the U-boat that had just attacked them, heading toward

R.P. Resor burning after a torpedo hit her port side, courtesy of The National Archives.

R.P. Resor, courtesy of The National Archives.

the Jersey coast. The two crewmen were soon picked up by a Coast Guard cutter. The search for other survivors continued but none were ever found. Of the 41 merchant seamen and nine U.S. Navy Armed Guardsmen aboard, there were only two survivors; Able Seaman, John J. Forsdal and U.S. Navy gunners mate, Daniel L. Huey.

On February 28th, two days after the attack, the drifting wreckage was taken into tow by the Navy tugboat USS Sagamore. While hauling the burned-out ship north to New York, the R.P. Resor bottomed out. The Sagamore cut her tow free and watched as the Resor rolled over and sank.

The circumstances surrounding the destruction of the R.P. Resor and the loss of all but two of her crew was considered the worst tragedy of an American merchant vessel during the war. The torpedoing also created a sensational impact upon the thousands of people on the Jersey coast. As they stood on the beach and watched the flames and smoke rising from the doomed ship they wondered if the war was starting to hit home.

Today, the Resor rests on the bottom, approximately 33 miles northeast of the Barnegat Inlet in 130 feet of water. Although the ship is still in one piece it appears to have been broken in two because of the drifting sand that has covered her deck midships. When most dive boats visit the Resor, they may charge an additional fee because of the distance from port. The dive should only be made by experienced deep divers due to the depth and the deteriorating condition of the wreck.

The tanker is an interesting dive with good lobster hunting and many artifacts. To the fisherman the R.P. Resor is best known for shark fishing. During the month of June, fishermen along the Jersey coast make the trip out to the wreck in hoping to land a mako. On one occasion, a dive boat was greeted by a 10 foot great white which refused to leave. Needless to say, there was no diving on the Resor that day. The wreck also offers excellent chances at cod, pollock and blackfish. Tuna are found here from June to October.

S.S. Rusland on the beach off Deal.

S.S. RUSLAND

BUILT: 1872
VESSEL TYPE: PASSENGER
  FREIGHTER
LENGTH: 345 FEET

LOST: MARCH 17, 1877
DEPTH: 25 FEET
LOCATION: 26950.2/43598.8

The Red Star Line steamer, S.S. Rusland, forced ashore by high winds, heavy seas and poor visibility, struck ground some 50 yards from the beach. Two days later it was discovered that the vessel was badly damaged, resulting in the removal of the 120 steerage passengers and the request of assistance from Life Saving Stations #4 and #6. It was believed that the ship had struck a rock.

On the morning of the 20th, a derelict barge arrived on the scene and set up a pump to remove the two feet of water in the stranded steamer's hold. Little progress was made and it was soon discovered that the ship was stuck fast onto the sunken vessel Adonis which came ashore twenty years earlier.

After most of the cargo was removed by surf boats and transported to Philadelphia, numerous attempts were made to free the Rusland from the sunken hulk. During the night of March 22, 1877, however, a strong northeast gale drove the freighter further into the sunken wreckage of the older wreck. She finally broke apart and fell beneath the surface. Only scattered wreckage of the Rusland remained above the water to mark its shallow water grave.

The steel steamship and the wooden bark make up today what are known as the "Dual Wrecks," located off the beach in Long Branch. The site is accessible by beach but it is more convenient to dive from a boat. The area these two ships encompass is enormous. It is an interesting dive site because the depth is shallow and there are two vessels.

Fishing over the "Dual Wrecks" will not go unrewarded. On any given day there are schools of small seabass, usually enough to prepare a good meal. Summer flounder will also be found in the area. Infrequently a diver will capture a lobster of legal size.

SALEM

BUILT: 1900
VESSEL TYPE: BARGE
LENGTH: UNKNOWN

LOST: APRIL 3, 1932
DEPTH: 55 FEET
LOCATION: 27008.4/42863.3

   The cause of the wreck of the Salem has never been revealed. The three men who made up the skeleton crew on the barge took that secret with them to their grave. A small column that appeared in the "New York Times" listed the three men as missing after their barge sank with no apparent cause.

   Today the remains of the Salem rest in 55 feet of water, eight miles due east of Townsend Inlet. Her wooden structure has given in to the sea, thus she now lies broken apart. Her decking can be easily identified and makes up the largest portion of the wreckage.

   She lies low to the bottom and may be difficult to locate. Fish appear to be scarce, probably because of her low profile.

USS SAN DIEGO

BUILT: 1903
VESSEL TYPE: U.S. NAVY
  CRUISER
LENGTH: 503 FEET

LOST: JULY 19, 1918
DEPTH: 100 FEET
LOCATION: 26543.3/43692.9

The heavy armored cruiser, USS San Diego, was commissioned originally as the California but was renamed seven years later when a much larger battleship was being built and was to be named after the Western states. The recommissioned San Diego, after being refitted, was 503 feet in length with a 69.5 foot beam and a displacement of 15,138 tons. Her top speed of 22 knots is indicative of the power delivered by her massive engines.

The armament on the cruiser was impressive as well. There were fifty cannons of varous sizes; four eight inch, fourteen six inch, eighteen three inch, twelve three pounders and two one pounders. She also had the capability to launch torpedoes and had four additional .30 caliber machine guns on deck.

With World War I moving close to home off the Atlantic coast, the San Diego was assigned to protect merchant shipping. The 1,200 crew members aboard the San Diego endured over a year without encountering the enemy. She escorted convoys up and down the coast and across the Atlantic.

Late one morning in July of 1918 she was on a routine mission when a lookout spotted an object in the water moving at a high rate of speed. This was reported to the bridge but nothing became of it. One hour later off the coast of Long Island a major explosion rocked the San Diego. A massive hole was torn in her port side, knocking out her port engine.

In a display of panic, sailors fired upon anything real or imagined while internal explosions continued to destroy the cruiser. In an effort to save his ship, Captain H.H. Christy, ordered full steam ahead with his starboard engine. Unfortunately this caused the sea water to flow into the gaping hole at a much greater rate than could be expelled by the bilge pumps. As it became evident that the San Diego would not stay afloat much longer, Captain Christy gave the order to abandon ship. Filling with water, it listed to port, rolled over and sank to the bottom. Of the twelve hundred crewmen aboard the cruiser all but six survived the catastrophe.

USS San Diego, courtesy of the U.S. Navy.

Today the remains of the San Diego lie upside down in 100 feet of water. Penetration must be made through the hull of the wreck. Each year there is more deterioration of the thick hull plates that increases access areas available to divers. All types of artifacts are recovered from the wreck including ammunition, medical supplies, guns, china, flatware, personal effects and nautical items.

A diver can retrieve a seafood feast with little effort. The wreck is a year-round haven for shellfish with an abundance of lobster, crabs, mussels, scallops and clams in and about the wreck site. Fish are also plentiful during most seasons including cod, seabass, porgies and blackfish. The San Diego's location is seven miles off Fire Island which makes it accessible to vessels of all sizes. For this reason, fishermen and divers are readily available to report on conditions.

San Jose, courtesy of The Steamship Historical Society, University of Baltimore Library.

SAN JOSE

BUILT: 1904
VESSEL TYPE: FREIGHTER
LENGTH: 330 FEET

LOST: JANUARY 17, 1942
DEPTH: 110 FEET
LOCATION: 26877.5/42955.4

With the German wolfpack traveling up and down the East Coast, it was necessary to implement "blackout" conditions, the running with no navigational lights, on all coastal shipping.

On the night of January 17, 1942, the 330 foot San Jose, bound for New York, collided with the Santa Elisa, 30 miles southeast of the Barnegat Inlet. The collision which took place around 8:00 p.m. on Saturday evening, sent the United Fruit ship freighter to the bottom in a matter of minutes. All of the forty crew members aboard escaped death when they were rudely thrown into the cold winter Atlantic.

Today the remains of the San Jose lie thirty-two miles southeast of the Barnegat Inlet, three miles north of the Atlantic City reef. The wreck rests in 110 feet of water and rises to within 70 feet of the surface. The wreckage of the San Jose is nearly intact and forms an excellent dive site. As with most wrecks in South Jersey the freighter is home to many bottom dwellers and fishermen can expect good catches through the entire year.

San Saba, courtesy of The Peabody Museum of Salem, Massachusetts.

SAN SABA

BUILT: 1879
VESSEL TYPE: FREIGHTER
LENGTH: 306 FEET

LOST: OCTOBER 4, 1918
DEPTH: 80 FEET
LOCATION: 26853.2/43240.6

Shortly before 1:00 a.m. on Friday, October 4, 1918, the American cargo steamer, San Saba, struck a mine fifteen miles southeast of the Barnegat Inlet.

The freighter was commanded by Captain Bergan Birdsall and maintained a crew of 37 men. She left the port of New York on October 3rd, bound for Tampa, Florida with a general cargo of 2,500 tons. One day out of port she struck the mine laid by a German submarine and the ill-fated freighter broke in two. Of the 37 crew members aboard only three survived.

The San Saba was built in 1879 at the Chester Boat Yard in Philadelphia, Pennsylvania. She was a 306 foot, single screw steamship. Originally named the Colorado, she was later renamed when she was gutted by a severe fire and had to be refurbished. The wreck of the San Saba is considered by many to be one of the most picturesque dive sites out of Barnegat Inlet. She rests in two sections, a few hundred yards apart. The stern piece, lying in eighty feet of water, is known as the "Magnolia", a nickname because of the anti-friction metal it was carrying, called magnolia bars. These bars are still being recovered by scuba divers. The bow section, unlike the stern, was never given a nickname. This section of the vessel also lies in eighty feet of water but only rises a few feet off the bottom since it was cleared for safe navigation. Both pieces are only seven miles from the Barnegat Inlet and are visited often.

Giant blackfish are known to inhabit the wreck and good size seabass. According to one fisherman who frequents the waters above the stern piece, eight to ten pound blackfish are easily caught using green crab. The seven mile journey to the San Saba is always worth the ride.

Sandy Hook

SANDY HOOK

BUILT: 1902
VESSEL TYPE: PILOT BOAT
LENGTH: 168 FEET

LOST: APRIL 27, 1939
DEPTH: 80 FEET
LOCATION: 26908.3/43700.4

The following information was acquired from the "New York Times" report of April 28, 1939. "In a thick fog that covered the entire area at 6:24 a.m., the incoming Norwegian liner, Oslofjord rammed the pilot boat, Sandy Hook, one mile outside the Ambrose Channel entrance when the pilot boat crossed the liner's bow. Thirty men aboard the Sandy Hook were saved and less than an hour later their vessel went down."

The accident was considered avoidable. In the dense fog the pilot boat was weaving through the boat traffic looking to deploy the twenty pilots she carried. The Oslofjord proceeding at dead slow speed, could do nothing when the pilot boat appeared out of the fog.

The remains of the 361 gross ton vessel lie in 80 feet of water just east of the Ambrose Light. Due to the muddy bottom, at times visibility can be reduced to nothing; at other times you can see forty feet. The stern section remains relatively intact but the midsection to the bow has been demolished. The wreckage rises as much as twenty feet in the stern to as little as five feet at the midsection. Although the site is not known for its fishing, it is always worth a try. Because of the location and visibility the wreck is not dove very often, therefore artifacts and lobster are plentiful to those lucky and persistent few.

SEA GIRT WRECK

VESSEL TYPE: SCHOONER
DEPTH: 80 FEET
CONSTRUCTION: WOOD
LOCATION: 26860.5/43471.6

The sunken schooner called the Sea Girt Wreck is well known to underwater photographers. Her remains are largely scattered over the bottom and give the eerie appearance of a pirate ship gone under. The schooner rises off the bottom twenty feet in some areas and ten feet in most. In the bow of the wreck her anchor chain lies piled as it would have been while sailing. Follow the chain to its end and you will come to a beautiful "popeye" style anchor set in the sand, as if holding the wreck in place. The anchor is an excellent backdrop for photos. The Sea Girt Wreck appears to have the dimensions of a football field. As is common with many wrecks in the North Atlantic, visibility can range from ten to one hundred feet.

Although the wreck has never been identified, artifacts recovered suggest that the vessel is circa 1900. Some of the artifacts include bottles, flatware and china, all originating from this time period.

Marine life is a large attraction to the site. Seabass, blackfish, ling, sea robin, eel pout, bergall and headfish inhabit the area in masses. Lobster, crab, scallop, mussel and clam are found in and around the wreck. The wooden remains are covered by a heavy growth of coral and barnacles.

SINDIA

BUILT: 1887
VESSEL TYPE: FOUR MASTED
  SCHOONER
LENGTH: 329 FEET

LOST: DECEMBER 15, 1901
DEPTH: 5 TO 10 FEET
LOCATION: 16TH STREET,
  OCEAN CITY

The following information about the sinking of the Sindia was supplied by The Friends of the Ocean City Historical Museum, located in Ocean City, New Jersey. Their help is appreciated.

In 1887 the keel of a steel vessel of 3,068 tons was laid in the yard of Harland & Wolff in Belfast, Ireland. One year later she sailed out of Victor Channel into Belfast Lough under the command of Captain MacKenzie. She was considered one of the finest ships ever produced in that harbor and her rig was that of a four-masted barque built for cargo carrying rather than for speed. She engaged largely in East Indian and Chinese trade and sailed a record of 200,000 miles.

She was a graceful ship with raked masts, and was built for, and owned by, the Brocklebank Shipping Company. The Sindia usually sailed between Liverpool and Calcutta with a crew of 36. She was registered in Liverpool and one year before she was wrecked, she was sold to the Anglo-American Oil Company.

After delivering a cargo of oil in China, she sailed to Kobe, Japan to load for her return trip to the United States. Bound for New York, she was laden with a cargo of camphor, silk, matting oil and novelties. She departed in July, 1901 and sailed south around Cape Horn, then northward along the coast, a journey of 10,000 miles, without mishap.

As she sailed north, a severe storm developed and on Sunday morning, December 15, 1901, she found a resting place upon the Ocean City, New Jersey beach. The Sindia was running west when she struck ground, but the wind turned her to the south. The vessel lay broadside within 150 yards of the shore, her bow pointing slightly to the southwest.

At half past two in the morning, signals of distress were seen by Mr. Harry Young and Mr. Edward Boyd of the Ocean City and Middle Station Life Saving Service. They responded with costin lights and then reported immediately to their respective stations. The two crews hurried to the scene, taking with them the breeches buoy

Sindia aground on the beach at Ocean City.

and Middle's surf boat. After three attempts to secure the buoy to the stranded schooner it was apparent that this method would not be successful.

At daybreak a surf boat was launched, manned by Captain J. Macket Corson of the Ocean City Station, and A.C. Townsend of the Middle Station, with a crew of 15 brave men. The wind blew at nearly hurricane levels and the rain swept down in torrents as they started for the helpless ship.

The surf boat could only creep slowly out over the angry sea, sometimes poised on the crest of a breaker, and then plunging forward into the trough of the sea that hid it from view. The boat would emerge again a few feet farther on, or from a cloud of spray and foam as the brawny arms of the seamen gave the forward or reverse stroke at the command of Captain Corson, standing in the stern and steering the craft.

The surf boat finally reached the Sindia. The captain at first refused to allow anyone to leave the ship, but he finally permitted the 26 men to depart. Seven men were taken on each trip. The sea continued to rage and the cold became so intense that after all of the crew was removed, the rescue efforts were abandoned.

The vessel and cargo were first taken charge by representatives of New York underwriters, and a wrecking company was given the job of unloading the vessel. Much of the cargo was taken out by divers and sold at the old Sindia store on the boardwalk. The expense of this operation, however, proved too great and a large part of the ship's valuable freight remains undisturbed by the hand of man.

The remains of the rudder post and tiller may still be seen above the sands at 16th Street beyond the boardwalk. Those who would like to learn more and see artifacts recovered from the Sindia, may visit the Ocean City Historical Museum located in Ocean City, New Jersey.

George R. Skolfield stranded on the beach at Sea Isle City.

GEORGE R. SKOLFIELD

BUILT: 1885
VESSEL TYPE: THREE
  MASTED SCHOONER
LENGTH: 232 FEET

LOST: FEBRUARY 5, 1920
DEPTH: 5 FEET
LOCATION: LUDLAM BEACH,
  SEA ISLE CITY

The George R. Skolfield was built in 1885 by the Skolfield Brothers of Brunswick, Maine who had a large fleet of vessels all named after family members, and this schooner was the largest of their fleet. Registered at 1,645 net tons, she was 232 feet in length, had a 40 foot beam and a hull draft of 25 feet. For fifteen years the schooner carried cargo to places such as the Far East and Hawaii. She also made routine trips up and down the East Coast.

At the turn of the century, steamships were becoming prevalent along the coast for transporting cargo. For this reason the much slower George R. Skolfield was sold to the Seaboard Company and was refitted into a schooner barge.

While being towed to Philadelphia, Pennsylvania with two other barges, the Skolfield broke free and washed ashore on Ludlam Beach off Sea Isle City. Her crew of four were rescued by the men of the Life Saving Station who put out in a surf boat. The schooner barge however, was a total loss.

For many years the wrecked vessel sat on the beach in five feet of water, disturbed only by those who ventured into the surf for a souvenir. Eventually the Skolfield broke apart and while some of her remains came ashore, much of the wreckage was left beneath the waves.

Today, scattered remains of the ship lie in the surf, five feet below the water. During low tide some of the wreckage actually sits out of the water. Although not a paradise for divers many fishermen consider striped bass fishing around the wreck to be above average.

Sommerstad dockside taking on cargo.

SOMMERSTAD

BUILT: 1906
VESSEL TYPE: FREIGHTER
LENGTH: 340 FEET

LOST: AUGUST 12, 1918
DEPTH: 165 FEET
LOCATION: 26425.0/43456.1

The Sommerstad was a Norwegian freighter built in New Castle, England in 1906. She was constructed of steel and had a displacement of 3,875 gross tons. In ballast from Norway to New York, the Sommerstad was cruising eleven knots some thirty miles off Long Island, New York. It was eight o'clock in the morning when a lookout on the bow reported a torpedo coming toward the starboard bow. It seemed the torpedo was going to miss the ship but suddenly, it turned and struck her port side.

Instantly, the Sommerstad started to go down by the stern. Lifeboats were launched and all crew members abandoned the sinking vessel. All thirty-one aboard were spared their lives. The men started rowing toward shore, and for over eleven hours they headed toward the coast when finally they were spotted by a patrol boat and rescued.

A report taken from the log book of a German submarine commander after the war stated that the U-117 was responsible for the sinking of the Sommerstad.

Today the wreck of the Sommerstad, known locally as the "Virginia" lies in 165 feet of water, 35 miles southeast of Fire Island Inlet. She received her nickname, the "Virginia", when first discovered in the 1950s by Long Island charter boat captain, Jay Porter. An Italian patron on board heard the captain refer to the new wreck as a virgin wreck. Not quite comprehending what the captain meant, the man began calling the wreck the "Virginia." Thus when the time came to name this mystery wreck, Captain Porter decided on the "Virginia." The wreckage rises twenty feet off the bottom.

Fishing the Sommerstad is excellent. I fished the "Virginia" during a spring charter a few years back. Cod and pollock were pulled over the rail in the ten to twenty pound range and within a few hours there were so many fish, the last few were thrown back. The wreck is well known to anglers and is considered a "hot spot." During each season, bottom dwellers, sharks, and/or the migrating tuna will surely be caught.

Stolt Dagali, courtesy of Skyphotos, Ashford, England.

STOLT DAGALI

BUILT: 1955
VESSEL TYPE: TANKER
LENGTH: 582 FEET

LOST: NOVEMBER 26, 1964
DEPTH: 130 FEET
LOCATION: 26787.6/43484.4

The Parcel lines tanker, Stolt Dagali, left Philadelphia on Thanksgiving evening, heading for Newark, New Jersey. It was a rainy night with calm seas and dense fog. At approximately the same time, the flagship of the Zim Lines, the Shalom, left the 80th Street Pier for its second transatlantic crossing. The 629 foot cruiser vessel was two years old and valued at twenty million dollars.

At 2:00 a.m., Thanksgiving morning, 23 miles northeast of the Barnegat Inlet, the Shalom struck the 582 foot tanker, cutting the Stolt Dagali in two. The stern sank instantly taking along nineteen of her crew members. Ten crew members including the captain remained aboard the floating bow section waiting for assistance. Twenty-three others were rescued by a lifeboat set out by the Shalom.

The Shalom, taking on water but in no danger of sinking, managed to make it back to New York. The bow section of the Stolt Dagali was put under tow from a Moran tug, and was also escorted by a Merrit, Chapman and Scott Corporation salvage vessel, the Curb. The bow section arrived in New York two days later and its cargo was off-loaded. The tanker was carrying industrial solvents, edible oils and fats.

Built in 1955, the Stolt Dagali sailed under the Norwegian flag. She was owned by A/S Ocean and managed by John P. Peterson and Sons of Oslo, Norway. Since no American vessel was involved in the collision, there was no U.S. inquiry. A spokesman for the Zim Lines reported in a later interview that the collision was caused by fog and an error in the radar room of the Shalom. A crew member had taken a wrong reading.

On December 2, 1964 two professional divers, James Caldwell of Toms River, New Jersey and Jack Brewer of Easton, Pennsylvania photographed the stern and estimated the wreckage to be at least 150 foot long. They also entered the engine room and some passageways but did not find any of the missing crew.

The stern section of the Stolt Dagali now rests with her port side rising 60 feet above the ocean floor in 120 feet of water. This is a good dive for both the new and experienced diver alike. The stern is fully intact and easily penetrated. Although it is not one of the better lobster wrecks, it makes up for this by nearly always having good visibility. Lack of hiding spots discourage most types of fish except the bottom dwellers. One interesting observation is that when tuna migrate close to shore, anglers will often anchor near the wreck to chunk for them. Artifacts are found within the wreckage and those penetrating the stern are often rewarded.

STONE BARGE

WRECK TYPE: BARGE
DEPTH: 55 FEET
CONSTRUCTION: WOOD
LOCATION: 26782.5/43728.2

The remains of the Stone Barge lie approximately three miles off Jones Inlet in 55 feet of water. The wreck was given its name because of the large granite rocks she was carrying.

According to diver/author, Dan Berg, from Long Island, New York, most of the wooden barge has either disappeared under the sand or deteriorated. The cargo of stones she was transporting make up most of the wreckage and provides safe haven to many fish and lobster. As Dan reported in his book "Wreck Valley II", on any given weekend during the summer, it isn't uncommon to see as many as ten boats anchored over her remains fishing for bottom species.

SUBMARINE S-5

BUILT: 1919
VESSEL TYPE: U.S. SUBMARINE
LENGTH: 231 FEET

LOST: SEPTEMBER 1, 1920
DEPTH: 170 FEET
LOCATION: 50 MILES EAST
OF CAPE MAY

The newly commissioned United States Navy submarine S-5 began maneuvers off the coast of New Jersey under the command of Lieutenant Commander Charles M. Cooke. Some fifty miles off the Cape May shore commander Cooke sounded the dive alarm and observed as the men took their stations.

Every crew member on board had a responsibility and Chief Gunners' Mate, Percy Fox, was to close the air induction valve when the diesel engines were stopped and power was switched over to electric. Warrant Officer Robert Holt, had given the command for the power switch, the bow planes were down, ballast tanks open, the submarine began her descent.

As the S-5 began her slow descent Commander Cooke realized that the air induction valve had not been closed. Water started to pour through the ventilation system as the crew scrambled to secure the valve. Cooke gave the order to surface and the crew quickly reacted to his command, but the submarine didn't respond. She continued to dive.

Before the induction valve could by fully closed the sub struck the bottom throwing the men about the submarine. Throughout the S-5 the sea water shorted out the electrical system and one of the two main motors cut out.

When the situation settled, Commander Cooke inspected the submarine to check on his men and to plan his next move. He noted that the integrity of the hull was water tight and the moral of his men was high.

The submarine was lying on the bottom in 170 feet of water, fifty miles east of Cape May, New Jersey and appeared to be the tomb for the 33 crewmen and four officers. Fortunately for the men, Commander Cooke didn't have it figured that way. Cooke felt that the S-5 being 231 feet in length and the depth being only 170 feet, if they were able to blow the aft ballast maybe they could raise the stern out of the water and attract a passing vessel. The problem however, was that the water going forward would eventually settle in the battery room and when sea water and sulfuric acid from the batteries mix they would produce deadly chlorine gas.

Seeing no other alternative Cooke gave the order to blow the aft ballast. Slowly as the stern began to lift toward the surface, water cascaded toward the bow sweeping with it any man or article that wasn't secured. As the sea water penetrated, the batteries' chlorine gas started to fill the battery room. The men scrambled to go aft which was above them, as now the stern rose quickly.

Making a rope from a curtain the crew members continued to climb up until they were above the battery room. The rest of the submarine was sealed off from the deadly gas.

Finally all 37 members of the crew aboard the S-5 made it to the stern of the submarine. If Commander Cooke was correct, the stern was now above water. To see if his theory paid off a drill was brought up and a 1/8" hole was cut threw the 3/4" steel hull. Seven hours after they first settled on the bottom, fresh air was once again flowing into the submarine.

For 30 hours the men of the S-5 used power drills, hand drills, hammers and chisel, the end result was a hole that measured 5 inches by 6 inches. Seeing that the men were exhausted and pace was too slow, Cooke abandoned the project. Instead they took a long piece of pipe with a shirt attached, raised it through the hole and waved the flag in hopes to be noticed.

As if following a text book, the next step unfolded. Out of nowhere the wooden freighter Atlantus appeared. Captain Edward Johnson had a lifeboat lowered and rowed over to the curious vessel. After a brief conversation between Johnson and Cooke the men aboard the freighter started the process to rescue these 37 captures. A cable was secured around the submarine to hold it in place and assure that it would not sink. A distress message was sent out and help was soon on its way.

On Friday, September 3, 1920, Commander Cooke was the last man to leave the submarine and board the battleship USS Ohio which was now present on the site.

Two Navy vessels, the USS Mallard and the USS Beaver were to take the sub in tow and bring her into port. After freeing her from the muddy bottom they started their forty mile journey home. Unfortunately the weather turned poor and the seas were building. The six inch towing cable split and the S-5 sank to the bottom. Several inspections and unsuccessful salvage attempts were performed by Navy divers. She was left in the environment she was made for.

The final resting place for the S-5 was discovered by a group of nautical historians and wreck divers. Divers Joe Milligan, Milt and Susan Herchenrider and Steven Sokoloff after a year and half of searching located the submarine in 1986. According to Milligan, he and the group of divers spent 18 weekends using a tow rope scanner, loran and depth recorder to search out over ten square miles before finding the sub. Joe noted that valuable information obtained by diver/author Gary Gentile and a tip from an anonymous boat captain aided in the S-5 discovery.

Joe said, "The S-5 lies in 170 feet of water, fully intact. She lists slightly to the port. Many artifacts have been recovered including; medicine bottles, sextant, silverware, dishes, gauges and a builder plaque bearing the name United States Submarine S-5."

Sumner, courtesy of the U.S. Navy.

SUMNER

BUILT: 1883
VESSEL TYPE: PASSENGER
   FREIGHTER
LENGTH: 351 FEET

LOST: DECEMBER 12, 1916
DEPTH: 25 FEET
LOCATION: 26916.8/43271.7

The U.S. Army transport ship Sumner was bound from the Panama Canal to New York City, carrying 199 soldiers, nine officers, thirteen prisoners and a few women and children passengers. At eleven o'clock on the last evening of the voyage, the weather conditions consisted of heavy seas and thick fog. Captain T.B. Webber, unsure of his location, posted extra watches, but shortly after, the vessel struck the sandbar off 12th Street in Barnegat. She struck so softly that only the people on the bridge knew that they were aground.

The next day, everyone was taken ashore with the help of the Revenue Cutter Mohawk and the Life Saving Stations of Barnegat City, Forked River and Loveladies. The Sumner was expected to be pulled free sometime during the next few days, but on the morning of December 22, 1916, after numerous attempts to free the ship, she broke at the seams and flooded. It was not long before the ocean took its toll on the doomed vessel and the ship tore apart.

The exact location of the Sumner has always been a point of controversy. Some local fishermen say that the remains of the wreck are often covered by the shifting sands around the Barnegat Inlet. Others contend that over the years the strong currents flowing in and out of the inlet have taken the remains of the Sumner with them. A few fellow divers who have dove what is believed to be the scattered wreckage of the freighter say that the dive is usually made with poor visibility and little reward.

Once a barge is positioned on the Artificial Reef it becomes home for vast schools of bait-fish and other bottom life. Photo by the Bureau of Marine Fisheries, Division of Fish, Game and Wildlife.

The chain of life that is attracted to an Artificial Reef is nearly endless and includes seabass which are usually plentiful. Photo by Pete Barrett.

SUNKEN DRY DOCK

VESSEL TYPE: BARGE
DEPTH: 60 FEET
CONSTRUCTION: WOOD
LOCATION: 26908.8/43506.8

Located in the vicinity of the Sea Girt Artificial Reef are the remains of a barge, known locally as the Sunken Dry Docks, reportedly sunk as part of the artificial reef program over twenty years ago. The barge now rests upright in 60 feet of water and rises fifteen feet off the bottom. There are few lobster, if any, on the wreck but schools of baitfish are often observed. For this reason bluefish occasionally cruise the area and can be found hovering above the remains. Fluke bury themselves in the sands around the wreck site, waiting for their prey.

This is an excellent site for novice and check-out divers. Visibility averages around ten feet, but can vary greatly depending on the surface conditions. The barge, fully intact, is approximately 150 feet long by 40 feet wide. Her preserved conditions makes it easy for divers to find their way around the wreck and return to the anchor with little difficulty.

Fishing for blackfish, seabass, ling and fluke can be very good and the wreck is a favorite of inshore anglers.

Texas Tower Number 4, courtesy of the U.S. Navy.

TEXAS TOWER NUMBER 4

BUILT: 1957
VESSEL TYPE: RADAR TOWER
LENGTH: UNKNOWN

LOST: JANUARY 15, 1961
DEPTH: 185 FEET
LOCATION: 26313.5/43266.6

The Texas Tower Number 4, an Air Force attack warning system, was taken out of service in September of 1960 when hurricane "Donna," which caused fifty foot seas and 130 mile an hour winds, knocked out the tower's radar system. Although not a ship, like many disasters, the tower was taken by the unpredictable sea.

After the storm, the Texas Tower was evacuated with the exception of fourteen civilians and fourteen crew members whose job it was to repair the radar station and keep it out of the hands of the Russians.

With winter approaching, the weather worsened as did the condition of the tower. Yet there was still no word from Air Force officials to evacuate the tower. Finally on January 15th, another devastating winter gale struck the tower. At that time, officials gave the word to evacuate. A Navy aircraft carrier was dispatched to the tower to remove the 28 people aboard. Traveling in a blinding storm while tracking the tower by radar, the ship was only thirty miles away when the Texas Tower disappeared from the radar screen. She collapsed and sank below the surface taking all twenty-eight men with her.

Today, the Texas Tower rests on the bottom, 75 miles off Barnegat, New Jersey. The wreckage lies in 185 feet of water, but rises to within 90 feet of the surface. The wreck is far from shore, which results in visibility exceeding one hundred feet and warm gulf stream waters. Every year dive boats make special trips to take divers to visit this blue water grave. The tower is a well known fishing area. Tuna, billfish, shark and nearly every type of wreck fish imaginable can be caught on the wreck when in season.

Texel, courtesy of The Steamship Historical Society, University of Baltimore Library.

TEXEL

BUILT: 1913
VESSEL TYPE: TANKER
LENGTH: 331 FEET

LOST: JUNE 6, 1918
DEPTH: 250 FEET
LOCATION: 26501.1/42796.2

Although the Texel is not a wreck that many divers frequent, the fishing is excellent and the story of its demise is an exciting one.

During World War I, German submarines made their biggest impact on merchant shipping on "Black Sunday," June 2, 1918. Two U-boats, the U-37 and U-151, sank eleven ships before moving southward.

The Texel was carrying a cargo of 42,000 tons of sugar from Puerto Rico, on a northern course bound for New York when confronted by one of the subs. According to New York Times coverage of the event, Captain K.B. Lowry of the Texel was quoted as saying:

"Suddenly, without a moment's warning, a U-boat loomed up off the bow. It fired three rounds of shrapnel. The hail of exploding shells swept the deck like rain. The U-boat was 50 feet away. So close that it almost crashed into the lifeboats that were lowered.

"When the shrapnel struck us, I stopped. The skipper of the U-boat came aboard and speaking clear English cried, 'Let me see your papers.' I turned the ship's papers over to him. He looked at them for a moment curtly, then turning on his heels said: "We will give you time to get off, then we shall sink your vessel.' "

An officer of the Texel was said to have overheard the German commander exclaim the following:

"I hate to do this. I used to command an American Liner and I have some good friends among the commanders of American steamers. I commanded big American Liners before we started this fuss, but war is war, so we will go through with this little job."

Immediately following these words, two lifeboats were lowered and all thirty-six crew members boarded and rowed away from the doomed vessel. Bombs were placed on the hull of the Texel just below the water line, and all watched from a distance as the vessel was destroyed and sank below the surface.

Today the fully intact hulk of the Texel rests in 250 feet of water, some 68 miles southeast of Barnegat Inlet. It is unknown whether this site has ever been dove, but it is said to be a hot spot for fishing and sharks, tuna, billfish and bottom fish are found on the wreck.

S.S. Thurmond, courtesy of William Gregor.

S.S. THURMOND

BUILT: 1890
VESSEL TYPE: HUMP BACK
  STEAMER
LENGTH: UNKNOWN

LOST: DECEMBER 25, 1909
DEPTH: 14 FEET
LOCATION: 200 FEET OFF
  "D" STREET IN
  SEASIDE PARK

While pulling three schooner barges loaded with coal to New York, the Standard Oil steamer, S.S. Thurmond, was forced to cut loose her tow when a Christmas day storm struck north of Seaside Heights, New Jersey. After cutting the three barges free, she went back to pick up the five crew members assigned to each barge. Only the first five crew members were rescued before all three barges sank. The other ten men were never found.

While looking for survivors in the blinding snowstorm, the steamer herself ran aground on the bar just off Seaside Park, where the vessel remained through the night. The next morning when beach master Captain Henry Ware of Toms River made his morning rounds, he spotted the vessel and called his men to assist in the rescue. They thought they would be able to pull the ship off the bar as soon as the tide was high enough. Before this could happen the vessel broke apart and sank.

The Thurmond's name was uncovered during the summer of 1984 when Ed Eglentowicz, Joe Paola and a few other divers, including the author, put in many hours of research to uncover this information. This history of the ship, known before only as the "Boiler Wreck," is still not totally complete. Many questions remain unanswered such as why a lake-going steamer with a rounded deck and very shallow beam was towing three barges in the unpredictable Atlantic, as well as the whereabouts of the three lost barges.

We do, however, know the whereabouts of the Thurmond. The wreck is located 200 feet off the beach in Seaside Park, New Jersey. Its two boilers are very easy to locate and make up the largest pieces of the wreck. Most of the ship has been swallowed up by the sea or buried under the sand, nevertheless, many small pieces of the wreck have been exposed over the years. The remains of the ship lie in 14 feet of water which is a great depth for both snorkeling and scuba diving. In the spring, blackfish and ling can be found, and on occasion a few small lobster.

197

Tolten, courtesy of the U.S. Coast Guard.

TOLTEN

BUILT: 1938
VESSEL TYPE: FREIGHTER
LENGTH: 280 FEET

LOST: MARCH 13, 1942
DEPTH: 90 FEET
LOCATION: 26815.9/43360.1

The Tolten was the only casualty of World War II for the South American country of Chile. She began her voyage from the Delaware Bay at 2:00 p.m. on March 12th, with her navigational lights on. Shortly before midnight the vessel was stopped by a U.S. Navy patrol boat and was instructed to travel without lights and to stay close to the coast. She was heading in ballast on a northerly course toward New York.

Twelve hours later, approximately fourteen miles northeast of Barnegat Inlet, two torpedoes ripped into her side. Without warning the ship was torn apart, sending her to the bottom in a matter of six minutes. There was not even time to lower a lifeboat. All crew members aboard except one were taken down with the ship.

The only survivor, Julio Faust, clung to a life raft for nearly twelve hours until rescued by a Coast Guard vessel.

One of his shipmates had spoken earlier of seeing a big black shadow to the seaward side of the Tolten. Faust was in his cabin when the torpedo struck and was saved only because the violent explosion threw him clear of the sinking vessel.

At the time of the sinking, Chile was a neutral country. The Chilean government had been assured by Germany, Italy and Japan that none of their ships would be endangered if they traveled with running lights. Needless to say, Chile felt the United States was responsible for the sinking.

The deteriorating remains of the Tolten lie in 90 feet of water and rise to within 50 feet of the surface. The steel hull can be easily penetrated but this is not suggested due to the condition of the wreckage. The site is sixteen miles from both Manasquan and Barnegat Inlets.

Many artifacts, as well as lobster, have been taken from the wreck. Fishing is rewarding as well with bottom fish and pelagics like blues and tuna in residence during the summer. The wreckage has a high profile and the bottom fish cover almost all levels. The abundance of summer flounder causes one to believe that this might be a breeding area and permanent home.

Varanger, courtesy of the U.S. Coast Guard.

VARANGER

BUILT: 1925
VESSEL TYPE: TANKER
LENGTH: 470 FEET

LOST: JANUARY 25, 1942
DEPTH: 130 FEET
LOCATION: 26825.3/42803.7

The 9,305 gross ton tanker, Varanger, was carrying a cargo of fuel oil to be off-loaded in New York Harbor. She was just a few short hours from her destination, when she fell victim to a German U-boat.

According to a New York Times report from January 26, 1942, three torpedoes from a U-boat struck the Norwegian tanker thirty-five miles off New Jersey. She went to the bottom quickly but the entire crew of forty managed to escape.

"The ship was struck at 3:10 a.m. by a torpedo amidship on the port side. The force of the explosion knocked the radio room and a four-inch gun overboard. Seven minutes later the ship was struck by a second torpedo. Five minutes later a third torpedo struck, the ship sank immediately after the third torpedo."

After the sinking the forty crew members were rowing toward shore in two lifeboats, one motorized, towing the other. They were rescued by the commercial fishing boat San Gennaro of Captain Morchetti. When he realized the men were in danger and needed help, he took those who were injured aboard, and began towing the remaining men in the lifeboats toward Townsend Inlet. A second fishing vessel, the Eileen, rendered further aid by towing one of the lifeboats. Once they reached shore, the Coast Guard took over the rescue operation.

The final resting place of the Varanger is in 130 feet of water, approximately 28 miles from the Absecon, Brigantine, Great Egg and Townsend Inlets hence the nickname, the "28 Mile Wreck." The area is a well-known fishing hot spot. Bluefish, tuna, bonito, skipjack and dolphin are caught in season. Codfish can be found year-round, but bite best in the spring and fall. During the warmer months, sharks inhabit the wreck and attract fishermen in pursuit of mako.

Joe Milligan recovered the bell of the Varanger in August of 1983.

Joe Milligan who dove the Varanger on numerous occasions and has recovered the ship's bell, describes the wreck as lying east to west. The bow is resting on her starboard side. Just to the back of the bow is a low lying area with extensive damage. The midsection, largely intact, consists of the bridge which rises 60 feet off the bottom. The stern has collapsed due to deterioration, but still rises well off the bottom. While diving off the Deep Adventures II, captained by John Larsen, an unmarked bell was recovered from the stern.

Early spring trips to the Varanger can usually produce some nice codfish. Photo by Captain Paul Regula.

A drawing of the lost steamship Vizcaya.

VIZCAYA-
CORNELIUS HARGRAVES

BUILT: 1872
VESSEL TYPE: PASSENGER
  FREIGHTER
LENGTH: 287 FEET

LOST: OCTOBER 30, 1890
DEPTH: 80 FEET
LOCATION: 26854.6/43295.2

BUILT: 1889
VESSEL TYPE: 4-MASTED
  SCHOONER
LENGTH: 211 FEET

LOST: OCTOBER 20, 1890
DEPTH: 80 FEET
LOCATION: 26854.8/43296.9

On a very clear night the Cuban ship, Vizcaya, better known as the "Spanish Steamer," was heading south, thirteen miles east of Barnegat. She was a large sail/steam vessel, traveling under steam power at that time due to the strong southerly winds. Most of the 90 passengers and crew had retired to their quarters for the evening.

At the same time, the 1,332 ton collier, Cornelius Hargraves, was heading north, traveling quickly and quietly through the water. Though the reason is unknown, the Hargraves was sailing with neither navigational lights or lookouts. The Vizcaya, with proper lights and a lookout posted, did not see the collier until a collision was unavoidable. The collier smashed into the Vizcaya's midsection, ripping the ship's timbers apart and she began to sink immediately. The collier, with its bow badly damaged, was also taking on water and in danger of sinking.

The captain of the Cornelius Hargraves put his pumps into action in an attempt to remove the water from his ship. After little success, he gave the order to abandon ship and lowered the lifeboats. The Vizcaya, on the other hand, was sinking so quickly that there was no time to lower the lifeboats. All ninety persons aboard were forced into the water.

Rescuers from the Hargraves lifeboats picked up survivors and rowed to the shore, leaving passengers from the Vizcaya clinging to a mast which remained above the water. The next day, those who still remained in the rigging were rescued by a passing ship. Fifty-three of the 90 passengers and crew lost their lives.

The Cornelius Hargraves in full sail.

The passenger freighter lies 80 feet below the surface and rises 20 feet off the bottom. It is possible to swim around its engines to take pictures of its large anchors in the bow. The Vizcaya site is known for artifacts which can be found in the territory around the wreckage.

The Hargraves rests less than one quarter of a mile from the Vizcaya. Her scattered remains rise only five feet off the bottom, thoroughly broken apart. It should be noted that some of the largest lobster captured have come from the wreck of the "Spanish Steamer." Divers will often make one dive on the steamer and a second on the collier. A greater concentration of fish, primarily ling, reside in the area surrounding the Hargraves.

WALCOTT WRECK

VESSEL TYPE: SCHOONER
DEPTH: 80 FEET
CONSTRUCTION: WOOD
LOCATION: 26518.1/43712.

The remains of a wooden schooner lie scattered six miles off Fire Island, New York. Nicknamed the Walcott, the bow is intact and rises ten feet off the bottom. The sunken schooner received her name because she was discovered on the day that Jersey Joe Walcott defeated Joe Louis in boxing.

To most divers and fishermen, the wreck of the Walcott is known only as a snag. On one particular dive, Captain John Larsen, captured a 35 pound lobster. On that same trip three more lobster of over 20 pounds were also taken.

Captain John Larsen with a 35 pound lobster taken from the Wolcott Wreck.

WAYNE

BUILT: UNKNOWN
VESSEL TYPE: BARGE
LENGTH: UNKNOWN

LOST: 1932
DEPTH: 45 FEET
LOCATION: 27033.9/42842.4

Approximately five miles southeast of Townsend Inlet off Avalon, New Jersey is the wreck of the Wayne. Very little is known about the events surrounding the sinking or if there were any casualties as a result.

The remains of the barge lie fully intact in 45 feet of water and she sits upright and rises 10 feet off the bottom. It is an excellent location for novice divers because of the depth and intact conditions of the wreck. As a result, returning to the anchor line is easily accomplished, even with the poorest visibility.

Visibility on the Wayne is usually good despite its distance from shore and shallow depth. This is partially attributable to the sandy bottom on which she lies, as well as the ambient light that penetrates the 45 feet of water.

The wreck is wooden and decaying, therefore creating many hiding areas for lobster. There are also plenty of fish on the Wayne as blackfish, seabass and bergall make their homes in the splintered remains. The fish tend to be school size of just one or two pounds, but are numerous on occasion.

A drawing of the Western World prior to her sinking.

WESTERN WORLD

BUILT: UNKNOWN

VESSEL TYPE: SAILING SHIP

LENGTH: UNKNOWN

LOST: OCTOBER 22, 1853

DEPTH: 35 FEET

LOCATION: 600 FEET OFF
THE BEACH AT
SPRING LAKE

The brig, Western World, bound for New York from Liverpool with three hundred passengers, came ashore north of Spring Lake, New Jersey in a heavy fog. The steam tug, Achilles, was dispatched to the scene and reported that the ship was lying with its bow to the north, broadside across the beach. There was seven feet of water in the hold of the Western World and she had lost her keel. The passengers had all been removed and taken to Sandy Hook.

Three days after the vessel had struck the bar, she was still stuck fast and there was now ten feet of water in her hold. In addition, she was being pushed by the sea further into the sand. On October 26th, four days after the Western World ran aground, it was reported that the vessel was no longer visible because it had apparently broken apart during the night and slipped beneath the waves.

Today, the remains of the Western World lie in a shallow grave of 18 feet of water, just beyond the surf off Spring Lake. Scuba divers have recovered many artifacts from the dive site including pewter, pottery and flatware.

WILLIAM B. DIGGS

BUILT: 1918
VESSEL TYPE: WOODEN BARGE
LENGTH: UNKNOWN

LOST: SEPTEMBER 3, 1934
DEPTH: 42 FEET
LOCATION: 27038.9/42746.1

The William B. Diggs, a 1,041 gross ton barge, was used as a salvage vessel along the Jersey coast by a local commercial dive firm. While attempting to salvage a shipwreck of unknown origin, the Diggs split at her seams and began taking on water. Within minutes the deck was awash. The crew immediately abandoned the barge and watched as she slowly slipped beneath the surface.

For more than forty years the barge rested peacefully offshore on the ocean floor with 42 feet of water over her decks. During this time a green blinker buoy marker was placed above the site to warn boaters of the danger below. Thus she acquired the nickname "Green Blinker Wreck." In the 1970s it was deemed necessary to demolish the remains of the Diggs as a navigational hazard. The wreck was cleared to rise only 15 feet off the bottom. The green blinker buoy, no longer needed, was later removed.

Today the remains of the wreck rest four miles off shore near Stone Harbor, New Jersey. The wreck is visited often by the local divers as a good training site for students. Lobster inhabit the wreck during the summer months as do seabass, summer flounder and bergall. A large fluke anchor resting on the bottom is an attraction for many photographers. Artifacts are still recovered from the wreck, but no one has yet uncovered the name of the mysterious vessel which lies below the Diggs.

WILLIAM R. FARREL

BUILT: 1900
VESSEL TYPE: TUG
LENGTH: 61 FEET

LOST: EARLY 1980s
DEPTH: 45 FEET
LOCATION: 26912.2/43240.5

The William R. Farrel has had many nicknames since she sank in the early 1980s. These have included the "Student Wreck." "Inshore Tug" and "NC Tug." The Farrel sank almost four miles southeast of the Barnegat Inlet off Harvey Cedars. Shortly after the sinking, Captain George Hoffman of the Sea Lion, made the first dive on her remains. He recovered many artifacts including the ship's bell.

Today the wreck of the Farrel sits upright with a starboard list. Her pilot house has been knocked off by a commercial fishing boat so the top of the vessel can be reached at twenty-five feet beneath the surface. The shallow depth makes this an excellent dive for students and novices. Visibility can be poor, but at the right times, underwater photography on this intact tug is rewarding. Small schools of bottom fish inhabit the wreck, although it is not a fisherman paradise.

YELLOW FLAG

VESSEL TYPE: SAILING SHIP
DEPTH: 75 FEET
CONSTRUCTION: WOOD
LOCATION: 26871.5/43230.6

Approximately eight miles southeast of Barnegat Inlet are the remains of a sailing ship known as the Yellow Flag. The wooden vessel lies broken open and is partially covered with sand from time to time. The wreckage is less than two miles inshore from the shipwrecks San Saba and Chaparra.

The Yellow Flag is not dove very often, perhaps due to the lack of historical knowledge. A few artifacts have been recovered from the site such as deadeyes, brass spikes and portholes, but none have helped to identify the vessel. Lobsters, scallops and mussels are found on and around the wreck. Fishing here may be difficult especially when much of her remains are buried. For this reason, there never appears to be many fish on the Yellow Flag.

APPENDIX

While researching the history of shipwrecks along the Jersey Coast, it was discovered that there were many interesting losses at sea. So many that a hundred books could be written on the subject. To demonstrate the profuse number, an alphabetical listing of sunken ships has been created. It covers the area from Shark River Inlet to Barnegat Inlet and dates back to as early as 1731.

A. FIELD
Bark, lost February 10, 1852. One life lost, wrecked off Deal.
A.H. BOWMAN
Schooner, lost December 4, 1857, off Deal.
A.H. DUMONT
Oil tanker, as part of the artificial reef program the vessel was sunk June 10, 1986, off Long Beach Island.
A.J. DONNELSON
Barque, lost February 19, 1835, wrecked off Manasquan.
A.M.C. SMITH
Schooner, lost October 13, 1876, off Manasquan.
ABBIE ABBOT
Schooner, lost January 20, 1903, off Ship Bottom.
ABERDEEN
Bark, lost 1855, on the Barnegat Shoals.
ABERDEEN
Bark, lost January 7, 1885. On voyage from Mobile, Alabama to Boston, wrecked off Barnegat Inlet.
ADDA J. BONNER
Barketine, lost February 7, 1880, off Barnegat.
AETNA
Schooner, lost December 3, 1830, off Manasquan.
AGENERIA
Schooner, lost December 7, 1838, off Mantoloking.
AGENORIA
Barkentine, lost December 7, 1839, outside the Barnegat Inlet.
AID
Schooner, lost August 3, 1864, off Barnegat.
AJI
Schooner, lost 1899, off Island Beach.
ALABAMA
Schooner, lost February 15, 1846, came ashore at Seaside Heights.

ALBERT W. SMITH
Schooner, lost April 11, 1894, ran aground at Manasquan.
ALBERTINE MEYER
Schooner, lost February 6, 1884, off Barnegat.
ALERT
Steamer, lost July 4, 1900, off Barnegat.
ALICE
Schooner, lost February 6, 1893, came aground off Ship Bottom.
ALKNAMOOK
Bark, lost January 4, 1876, off Long Branch.
ALTAVELE
Schooner, lost May 2, 1884, off Barnegat.
AMANDA WINANTS
Schooner, lost September 1874, off Barnegat.
AMERICA
Steamship, lost October 5, 1866. Bound for New York with a cargo of cotton, wrecked off Barnegat.
AMERICAN
Schooner, lost October 5, 1866, on the Barnegat Shoals.
AMITY
Schooner, lost March 1, 1861, off Manasquan.
AMITY
Ship, lost September 11, 1824, off Manasquan.
AMPHITRITE
Brig, lost February 26, 1832, off Barnegat.
ANASTASIA
Barge, lost 1931. The wreck lies nine miles off Seaside Heights in 70 feet of water.
ANASTASIA
Barge, lost January 26, 1933. Four lost when the vessel sank off Barnegat.
ANASTASIA
Freighter, lost during World War II, seven miles off Lavalette Beach.
ANDREW H. EDWARDS
Bark, lost June 28, 1888, off Island Beach.
ANDREW JACKSON
Ship, lost 1821, off Long Beach.
ANNA BROWN
Schooner, lost February 23, 1880. Wrecked off Island Beach in storm.

ANNADALE

Schooner, lost December 4, 1869, off Manasquan.

ANN CORBETT

Schooner, lost January 1870. On voyage from Baltimore with cargo of corn, wrecked off Manasquan.

ANNE RUBINE

Schooner, lost 1942. This small vessel came ashore during a gale, off Seaside Park.

ANNIE L. PALMER

Schooner, lost March 13, 1882. Foundered in Barnegat Bay, off Forked River.

ANONYMA

Schooner, lost November 4, 1883, off Manasquan.

ANTILLA

Barkentine, lost March 28, 1902, off Long Beach Island.

ANTIOCH

Barkentine, lost March 26, 1913. In transit to New York when the vessel came aground off Manasquan.

These nice blackfish were speared while diving a wreck off of Long Branch. Photo by Howard Rothweiler.

ARABELLA
Schooner, lost September 10, 1846. Seven crewmen drowned when she came ashore at Barnegat.

ARGYLE
Swedish bark, lost March 1852, three miles south of Manasquan.

ARGYLE
Bark, lost January 28, 1855. All those aboard were lost except one when she came ashore off Barnegat.

ARION
Bark, lost 1852, off Manasquan.

ARKANSAS
Schooner barge, lost January 28, 1928. All five crewmen aboard lost their lives when the vessel broke up near the Barnegat Lighthouse.

ARTIC
Schooner, lost November 23, 1881, off Mantoloking.

AUBURN
Bark, lost 1847, off Barnegat.

AURBURN
Schooner, lost 1870, came aground on the Barnegat Shoals.

AUSTRIA
Schooner, lost March 1877, off Manasquan.

B.C. SCHRIVINER
Schooner, lost May 5, 1870. Carrying a cargo of ice to be delivered in New York, she came ashore off the beach in Manasquan.

BALANCE
Ship, lost March 24, 1746, off Barnegat.

BELLE
Schooner, lost February 8, 1868, off Deal Beach.

BENEFACTOR
Schooner, lost February 19, 1902. Collided with the schooner Joseph J. Pharo off Island Beach.

BENJAMIN AND ELIZABETH
Ship, lost May 13, 1809, came ashore off Manasquan.

BERTHA WARNER
Schooner, lost November 30, 1896. Broke apart in the Barnegat Bay off Toms River when it struck a submerged object.

BESSIE YORK
Schooner, lost May 30, 1867, off Long Beach Island.

BETSEY
Brig, lost 1778, foundered in the breakers off Beach Haven.

BIANCA ASPASIA

Bark, lost May 23, 1901, off Ship Bottom.

BIRD

Steamship, lost December 1, 1855. Collided with the vessel Palmeto off Red Bank.

BLACK ARROW

Yacht, lost 1954, off Barnegat Inlet.

BLUEFISH

Motorboat, lost July 22, 1950, sank outside the Barnegat Inlet.

BOUNDING BILLOW

Schooner, lost April 3, 1883, on the Barnegat Shoals.

BREEZE

Steamship, lost October 16, 1876, off Long Beach Island.

BRISTOL

Schooner, lost September 4, 1910. Collided with the Italian steamship Dinnamare off Barnegat.

BRUNSWICK

Brig, lost November 1780, off Barnegat.

BURINE

Schooner, lost November 14, 1881, off Mantoloking.

C.C. DAME

Schooner, lost January 1884, off Bay Head.

C.E. JOHNSON

Schooner, lost December 24, 1875. In ballast to Philadelphia, she came aground at Deal Beach.

C. MATHEW

Schooner, lost September 9, 1865, off Manasquan.

CADDO

Barge, lost August 26, 1921, foundered seven miles off Barnegat.

CALEB. S. RIDGEWAY

Schooner, lost November 13, 1885. Wrecked in the Barnegat Bay off Toms River.

CAPE HENRY

Schooner, lost June 8, 1831, carrying a cargo of soap, came ashore off Manasquan.

CARISSA MADRE

Schooner, lost December 2, 1873, near Shark River.

CARISSSA MALTIE

Italian bark, lost December 2, 1873. With a cargo of chalk to be taken to New York, foundered off Shark River.

CAROLATTA
  Schooner, lost June 27, 1867. Loaded with coal to be delivered to Providence, Rhode Island, she came ashore off Manasquan.
CATERINA
  Italian bark, lost October 23, 1912, cargo of bones, off Barnegat.
CATONSVILLE
  Schooner, lost January 28, 1928. Four crewmen were lost when she foundered off Barnegat Lighthouse.
CECIL P. STEWART
  Schooner, lost February 17, 1927, south of Barnegat Lighthouse.
CHAIRES
  Schooner, lost 1856, off Barnegat.
CHALMETTE
  Steamer, lost July 28, 1913, cargo of lumber, off Barnegat.
CHARLES
  Bark, lost 1856, off Barnegat.
CHARLES E. POPE
  Schooner, lost May 8, 1867, off Manasquan.
CHARLES F. MAYER
  Schooner, lost October 20, 1887, off Chadwick Beach.
CHARLES HECKSHER
  Schooner, lost December 31, 1866, near Shark River.
CHARLES H. VALENTINE
  Schooner, lost October 29, 1885, off Barnegat.
CHARLES M. NEWINS
  Schooner, lost January 28, 1881, off Barnegat.
CHARLOTTE
  Schooner, lost December 9, 1931, off Sea Girt.
CHATTORA
  Cuban steamship, lost October 27, 1918, ten miles off Barnegat Inlet.
CHEASAPEAKE
  Steamship, lost May 14, 1913, off Barnegat.
CHRISTINE LOUISA
  Ship, lost March 26, 1832, off Manasquan.
CIENFUEGOS
  Schooner, lost May 27, 1922, foundered off Barnegat.
CINDERELLA
  Commercial fishing vessel, lost March 15, 1983, four miles east of the Manasquan Inlet.
CIRCASSIAN
  Schooner, lost December 21, 1869, off Manasquan.

CIVITAS CARRERA
Italian bark, lost June 28, 1888, wrecked off Manasquan. In a storm in 1937 the remains of the vessel were uncovered and a ton of brass was salvaged from the site.

CLARA
Schooner, lost January 12, 1922, foundered off Sea Girt.

CLARA BROOKMAN
Steamship, lost September 15, 1857, off Manasquan.

CLARA C. FRYE
Schooner, lost January 27, 1871, loaded with lumber, off Barnegat.

CODDINGTON
Brig, lost May 14, 1839, off Island Beach.

COLUMBIA
Schooner, lost January 17, 1828, off Deal.

COQUETTE
Steamship, lost March 24, 1868, stranded off Long Beach Island.

CORA
Schooner, lost November 8, 1875, cargo of poles, off Manasquan.

CORBELLA
Spanish bark, lost December 18, 1857, near Shark River.

CORDULA
Schooner, lost December 1867, cargo of coal, off Manasquan.

COSTA RICA
Brig, lost January 16, 1869 off Bay Head.

COUNTY OF EDINBURGH
Schooner, lost July 2, 1899, off Point Pleasant.

CRETANAN
Schooner, lost July 4, 1865, carrying a cargo of lime, off Barnegat.

CROATAN
Barge, lost October 8, 1940, foundered off Ship Bottom.

CUBA
Steamer, lost January 16, 1879, off Ship Bottom.

CYBELE
Schooner, lost September 11, 1879, off Manasquan.

D.C. BRADLEY
Schooner, lost February 22, 1878, off Manasquan.

D.W. SANDERS
Schooner, lost 1857, off Manasquan.

DAVID H. TOLCK
Schooner, lost February 22, 1879. Sailed from Maine and wrecked off Harvey Cedars.

Blackfish are not only a tough fish to hook but they are even more difficult to photograph. Photo by Herb Segars.

DE MOREY GRAY

Schooner, lost March 9, 1874, off Barnegat.

DE WITT CLINTON

Ship, lost November 4, 1860, off Manasquan.

DECEIVER

Sloop, lost March 29, 1884, on the Barnegat Shoals.

DIXIE

Fishing vessel, lost April 20, 1893, near Forked River.

E.H. ATWOOD

Schooner, lost May 30, 1878, off Deal.

E & C DAYTON

Sloop, lost October 21, 1875, cargo of oysters, wrecked at Deal.

EASTLAND

Steel vessel, lost September 1915, capsized and sank off Barnegat.

EDWARD EVERETT

Schooner, lost 1855, off Long Branch.

EDWARD TILTON

Schooner, lost June 12, 1903, off Island Beach.

EDWIN A. JAYNES

Schooner, lost May 22, 1888, off Barnegat.

ELMIRA

Schooner, lost January 1884, off Harvey Cedars.

ELIZA JANE

Schooner, lost September 17, 1876, off Seaside Heights.

ELIZABETH

Brig, lost January 10, 1820. Bound for New York with a cargo of cotton, foundered off Deal Beach.

ELIZABETH

Ship, lost May 13, 1864, 378 passengers and a cargo of iron, came ashore at Manasquan.

EMILY & JENNIE

Schooner, lost April 8, 1888, off Harvey Cedars.

EMMA D. BLEW

Schooner, lost August 18, 1879, off Long Beach Island.

ENTERPRISE

Schooner, lost March 8, 1835, off Cranberry Inlet which was located near Seaside Heights.

EQUATOR

Schooner, lost November 10, 1838, off Long Branch.

ERNA

German bark, lost September 13, 1889, cargo of lumber, on the Barnegat Shoals.

ESPERANZE

Schooner, lost 1864, wrecked off Point Pleasant.

ESSEX

Steamship, lost June 5, 1923, foundered off Beach Haven.

ESTELLA F.

Motor boat, lost October 22, 1916, off Barnegat.

ESTELLE PHINNEY

Schooner, lost December 27, 1907. Collided with the collier Elizabeth Palmer, off Barnegat.

ETNA

Schooner, lost February 8, 1830, off Manasquan Beach.

ETTA M. TUCKER

Schooner, lost January 31, 1878, wrecked off Asbury Park.

EUPHEMIA

Brig, lost February 18, 1885, off Mantoloking.

EVE

Schooner, lost May 8, 1867, off Asbury Park.

EVERETT PRESTO

Steamship, lost March 12, 1883, off Barnegat.

F.F. CLAIN
Barge, lost February 17, 1942, foundered off Barnegat.
FAIRMONT
Steamer, lost February 12, 1888, off Bay Head.
FANNIE
Schooner, lost March 6, 1872, cargo of corn, off Barnegat.
FAWN
Brig, lost April 1, 1854, off Deal.
FIVE SISTERS
Schooner, lost 1880, wrecked in the Barnegat Bay near Toms River.
FLASH
Schooner, lost January 3, 1880, off Barnegat.
FLORA
Bark, lost December 31, 1865, cargo of cotton, off Manasquan.
FLORA KIMBALL
Schooner, lost April, 10, 1915, cargo of lumber, wrecked off the Barnegat Shoals.
FLORENCE THURLOW
Schooner, lost May 12, 1920, collided with the S.S. Laramie off Sea Girt.
FORMOSA
Schooner, lost November 11, 1880, off Mantoloking.
FORTUNATO
Bark, lost 1851, off Manasquan.
FRANCIS HALLECK
Schooner, lost November 27, 1890. Collided with an unidentified schooner off Barnegat.
FRANCIS PERKINS
Schooner, lost 1887, near Toms River.
FRIENDSHIP
Brig, lost 1813, off Manasquan.
G. PORTER GRIFFITH
Schooner, lost October 12, 1866, cargo of lime, off Barnegat.
G.W. BARBER
Brig, lost August 7, 1867. Bound for New York with a cargo of sugar, foundered off Barnegat.
G.W. HINSON
Schooner, lost January 22, 1867, cargo of cotton, off Manasquan.
GARRICK
Schooner, lost January 26, 1847, off Deal.

GENERAL PUTNAM
Ship, lost January 31, 1832, off Island Beach.
GEORGE H. SCOTT
Schooner, lost April 23, 1883, off Deal.
GEORGE LEWMON
Schooner, lost April 23, 1883, off Deal.
GEORGE STEERS
Pilot boat, lost February 1865, five lives lost, off Barnegat.
GEORGE TULANE
Schooner, lost February 3, 1880, off Mantoloking Beach.
GEORGE WHITE
Schooner, lost October 17, 1883, off Barnegat.
GEORGIA
Schooner, lost 1845, off Long Beach Island.
GERMANIA
Bark, lost November 26, 1889, off Long Branch.
GILMAN D. KING
Schooner, lost June 2, 1870. With a cargo of bamboo from Jamaica, sank off Manasquan.

Using underwater scooters makes it easy for divers to cover more ground while making a dive. Photo by Herb Segars.

GLEANOR
Ship, lost 1840, cargo of hides, wool and fur, off Long Beach Island.

GLIDE
Schooner, lost March 15, 1867, off Barnegat.

GORDON
Sloop, lost December 30, 1874, cargo of raisins and potatoes, wrecked off Barnegat.

GOVERNOR BULL
Brig, lost May 4, 1861, cargo of sugar, off Manasquan.

GOV. CODDINGTON
Brig, lost May 14, 1938, off Island Beach.

GRACE
Schooner, lost January 12, 1922, foundered off Sea Girt.

GRACE DARLING
Schooner, lost January 5, 1856, off Long Beach Island.

GRAND TURK
Schooner, lost February 28, 1853, three crewmen lost, off Manasquan.

GREYHOUND
Brig, lost March 31, 1813, off Barnegat.

GUADALOUPE
Steamship, lost November 20, 1884, cargo of iron and gin. Broke in two on the Barnegat Shoals.

GWENNIE
Schooner, lost January 24, 1908, foundered off Barnegat.

H.R. CONGDON
Schooner, lost April 20, 1893, cargo of coal, off Deal.

HAROLD B. COUSINS
Schooner, lost January 9, 1911, on the Barnegat Shoals.

HALLOWELL
Schooner, lost August 18, 1830, off Island Beach.

HAMILTON FISH
Brig barge, lost March 6, 1906, caught fire and sank off Long Beach Island.

HANNAH ANN
Sloop, lost March 11, 1836, foundered off Manasquan.

HANNAH SPAULDING
Schooner, lost 1864, off Long Beach Island.

HARRIET ANDERSON
Schooner, lost August 22, 1829, sank in the Barnegat Bay near Tuckerton.

HARRIET NEWELL
Schooner, lost March 16, 1861, off Deal.

HARRISON JONES
Schooner, lost September 23, 1859, off Deal.

HARRY RUSE
Barge, lost February 17, 1942, 25 miles off Beach Haven. Believed to be a war victim.

HARRY RUSH
Freighter, lost February 17, 1943. She sank eight miles off Barnegat Inlet when she was struck by the F.F. Clain.

HATTIE S. COLLINS
Schooner, lost March 28, 1884, off Barnegat.

HAVANNA
Schooner, lost January 11, 1922, foundered off Mantoloking.

HAZARD
Brig, lost 1862, in the Manasquan Inlet.

HELEN
Brig, lost November 19, 1769, off Barnegat.

HELEN J. SEITZ
Five masted schooner, lost February 9, 1907, off Barnegat.

HELEN MAUD
Schooner, lost 1854, on the Barnegat Shoals.

HENDRIK HUDSON
Schooner, lost May 1865, cargo of coal, off Barnegat.

HENRY CLAY
Schooner, lost May 7, 1838, off Mantoloking.

HENRY DAVEY
Schooner, lost April 1892. Collided with the schooner O.D. Slamm off Manasquan.

HENRY FINCH
Schooner, lost November 27, 1897, off Harvey Cedars.

HENRY FRANKLIN
Schooner, lost March 17, 1834, off Barnegat.

HENRY GRATTAN
Ship, lost 1834. Sailed from Ireland carrying 350 immigrants, foundered off Long Beach Island.

HENRY R. CONDON
Steamer, lost April 20, 1893, off Deal.

HERBERT
Barge, lost September 30, 1944, foundered off Barnegat.

HESTER A. SEWARD
Schooner, lost June 26, 1896, off Chadwick Beach.

HOLLAND
> Bark, lost February 8, 1864. Bound for Curacao from New York, wrecked off Barnegat.

HOMEWARD BOUND
> Schooner, lost March 21, 1879, off Belmar.

HUNTER
> Brig, lost March 5, 1832, off Manasquan.

HYACINTH
> Schooner lost 1880, off Manasquan.

IDAHO
> Steamship, lost December 23, 1865, off Barnegat.

IMPERATIVE ELIZABETTA
> Bark, lost 1868, off Long Beach Island.

INDUSTY
> Schooner, lost June 20, 1773, off Barnegat.

IOU 1971
> Cabin cruiser, lost May 27, 1951, in the Barnegat Inlet.

IRENE
> Barge, lost May 26, 1934, off Barnegat Lighthouse.

ISAACE HITILLYER
> Schooner, lost October 28, 1889, off Forked River.

ITALIA
> Bark, lost January 16, 1879, off Deal.

J.C. RAHIMUS
> Bark, lost December 13, 1864, cargo of sugar, lost off Deal.

J.L. HOLMES
> Schooner, lost September 8, 1917. She struck the wreck of the Sumner off Barnegat Inlet.

J.R. STANLEY
> Schooner, lost November 5, 1859, off Manasquan Beach.

J.W. ELWELL
> Schooner, lost November 5, 1875, off Barnegat.

J.W. WENDT
> Ship, lost March 21, 1889, cargo of 13,000 barrels of oil and 400 tons of pig iron, wrecked off Barnegat.

JAMES ANDREWS
> Schooner, lost November 1862, off Barnegat.

JAMES B. JOHNSON
> Schooner, lost January 25, 1890, off Forked River.

JAMES CLEMENTIS
> Schooner barge, lost February 22, 1878, cargo of coal, wrecked off Deal Beach.

JAMES FISHER
Schooner, lost October 12, 1834, off Barnegat.

JAMES M. HALL
Schooner, lost November 15, 1906, stranded off Long Branch.

JAMES NELSON
Sloop, lost March 24, 1875. Sailing out of the Barnegat Inlet she struck the wrecked remains of the Idaho and sank.

JEFFERSON
Steamship, lost December 14, 1882, off Barnegat.

JEROME
British brig, lost December 22, 1856, cargo of molasses and salt, off Deal.

JEWESS
Steamship, lost November 11, 1854, stranded off Barnegat.

JOHN A. BRIDGES
Schooner, lost December 26, 1909, six lives lost, foundered off Barnegat.

JOHNATHAN MYER
Schooner, lost December 1835, off Manasquan.

JOHN B. MYERS
Schooner, lost November 1872, off Barnegat.

JOHN C. JACKSON
Schooner, lost 1840, off Manasquan Inlet.

JOHN F. KRANZ
Barge, lost March 21, 1903, off Mantoloking.

JOHN W. WINSTEAD
Schooner barge, lost December 5, 1927, foundered off Sea Girt.

JOHN SHERWOOD
Barkentine, lost October 27, 1886, cargo of ice, off Chadwick.

JOHN W. FOX
Schooner barge, lost June 29, 1900, off Spring Lake.

JOSEPH
Ship, lost December 17, 1809, off Manasquan Beach.

JOSEPH BANNIGAN
Barge, lost March 24, 1891, off Long Branch.

JOSEPH L. BELLOW
Schooner, lost February 1867, off Barnegat.

JOSEPH LONG
Schooner, lost March 16, 1870, off Long Branch.

JOSIE R. BURT
Schooner, lost August 30, 1911, foundered off Barnegat.

JUDGE BAKER
Schooner, lost 1860, no survivors, off Manasquan.

JULIA
Bark, lost February 4, 1882, in the Barnegat Bay.

JULIA A. BERKELE
Schooner, lost May 3, 1879, off Barnegat.

KARL JEVICA
Schooner, lost February 12, 1886, 10 of the 13 crew lost their lives, on the Barnegat Shoals.

KATE SMITH
Bark, lost February 1871, cargo of corn, off Barnegat.

KATHERINE DEMPSEY
Barge, lost April 7, 1910, cargo of lumber, wrecked off Spring Lake.

KNICKERBOCKER
Schooner, lost October 19, 1915, three lives lost, foundered off Barnegat.

KONG THRYME
Brig, lost 1856, on the Barnegat Shoals.

L & A BABCOCK
Barge, lost June 6, 1884, off Island Beach.

L. SARGENT
Bark, lost August 18, 1879, off Barnegat.

LA FAUVETTE
French bark, lost May 1849, off Manasquan.

LAKE GEORGE
Sloop, lost November 8, 1756, off Barnegat.

LA TIGRE
Brig, lost January 11, 1820, wrecked in a gale off Barnegat.

LAURA W.
Barge, lost March 28, 1903, off Chadwick.

LAURENCE McKENZIE
Schooner, lost March 21, 1890, cargo of oranges, off Forked River.

LEON WALTERS
Oilscrew vessel, lost March 23, 1964, collided with the S.S. Hess Bunker.

LESTER A. LEWIS
Schooner, lost March 30, 1889, off Long Branch.

LEWIS
Ship, lost March 6, 1827, off Manasquan Beach.

LEWIS MCLANE
Schooner, lost May 2, 1827, off Barnegat.

LIBERNO
French ship, lost April 25, 1863, off Shark River.

LIBERTY
Scallop boat, lost December 13, 1983, 2 lives lost, wrecked in the Manasquan Inlet.

LILLIAN CAMERONE
Brigantine, lost December 26, 1876, cargo of potatoes, off Manasquan Beach.

LIVE OAK
Sloop, lost October 20, 1769, cargo of sugar, 14 lives lost, off the Beach in Manasquan.

LIVERPOOL
Ship, lost 1791, on the Barnegat Shoals.

LIZZIE LANE
Sloop, lost February 24, 1873, off Manasquan.

LIZZIE MAUL
Schooner, lost June 6, 1875, cargo of railroad iron, wrecked off Deal.

LIZZIE WILSON
Schooner, lost August 18, 1887, collided off Barnegat.

LOCKWOOD
Schooner barge, lost July 10, 1867, cargo of coal, off Barnegat.

LOLA MAY
Brig, lost May 16, 1835, off Manasquan.

LORD WELLINGTON
Ship, lost 1847, off Barnegat.

LOVE AND UNITY
British ship, lost August 1, 1778, cargo including: 80 hogheads of loaf sugar, thousands of bottles of wine, Bristol beer, cider, flour, salt, cheese, flatware, wine glasses, other china. Vessel was lost off old Cranberry Inlet.

LULU AMMERMAN
Schooner, lost November 4, 1883, off Forked River.

LYDIA
Schooner, lost April 6, 1835, off Seaside Heights.

M.J. FORSHA
Sloop, lost September 17, 1875, cargo of potatoes, off Manasquan.

M.M. MERRIMAN
Schooner, lost November 17, 1869, off Manasquan Beach.

MAGDALINA
Brig, lost September 17, 1876, off old Cranberry Inlet.
MAGNUS
Brig, lost April 19, 1877, cargo of sugar, off Barnegat.
MAIDEN CREEK
Freighter, lost December 31, 1942, victim of war, off Shark River.
MALAY
Bark, lost June 10, 1858, off Barnegat Inlet.
MALOHA
Gas screw vessel, lost November 25, 1945, stranded off Asbury Park.
MARIA JEWELL
Schooner, lost February 14, 1855, off Deal.
MARIANO BEUVENETO
Italian bark, lost April 14, 1874, cargo of salt, wrecked off Barnegat.
MARIA PIERSON
Schooner, lost January 8, 1894, off Bay Head.
MARION
Barge, lost October 28, 1938, foundered four miles north of Manasquan.

This 10 pound blackfish was taken from the Persephone. Photo by Howard Rothweiler.

MARTHA E. MACCABE
Schooner, lost March 20, 1906, off Barnegat.
MARY
Brig, lost December 26, 1833, cargo of rice, off Manasquan.
MARY AND ELIZA
Schooner, lost February 14, 1832, off Manasquan Beach.
MARY C. DWYER
Bark, lost 1857, off Barnegat.
MARY C. TOWN
Schooner, lost February 1867, off Barnegat.
MARY E. MILLS
Schooner, lost May 23, 1921, cargo of oysters, off Barnegat.
MARY F. KELLY
Fishing schooner, lost August 24, 1893, off Deal.
MARY HALEY
Schooner, lost May 8, 1886, sank in the Barnegat Bay off Toms River.
MARY OF WINCAPET
Brig, lost April 1828, off Barnegat.
MASCOTTE
Schooner, lost September 17, 1885, off Forked River.
MASON DAVIS
Ship, lost September 22, 1859, off Deal.
MEDIATOR
Steamship, lost, January 22, 1875, off Barnegat Inlet.
MELODY
Schooner, lost July 3, 1886, off Barnegat Inlet.
MEMENTO
Bark, lost November 30, 1867, off Point Pleasant.
MERVAL
Schooner, lost January 24, 1828, off Island Beach.
META
Schooner, lost October 14, 1883, off Bay Head.
MILVILLE
Schooner barge, lost December 4, 1927, foundered off Sea Girt.
MINERVA
Ship, lost April 20, 1857, off Manasquan.
MOBILE
Brig, lost April 20, 1828, off Manasquan.

MOLA

British schooner, lost March 1901, off Chadwick Beach.

MONIO

Dutch brig, lost March 20, 1864, cargo of wood and skins, wrecked off Manasquan.

MORGANIA

Brig, lost 1837, off Barnegat.

MORNING STAR

Schooner, lost June 5, 1867, off Deal.

MORRO CASTLE

Steamship, lost September 8, 1934. Ship caught fire and burned four miles east of Belmar. Although she did not sink and was beached, 126 people lost their lives.

NEW ERA

Ship, lost November 13, 1854, 222 lives lost, off Asbury Park.

NEW YORK

Ship, lost January 26, 1856, off Barnegat Inlet.

NEWPORT

Barge, lost August 18, 1946, off Long Branch.

NIELLE S. JARRELL

Schooner, lost 1877, wrecked off Barnegat.

NORTHERN NO. 8

Barge, lost January 16, 1924, stranded off Long Branch.

NUMBER EIGHT

Schooner barge, lost July 20, 1916. Collided with the S.S. Comus off Sea Girt.

NUMBER TWENTY

Schooner barge, lost February 4, 1926, three lives lost, off Barnegat.

NUMBER TWENTY-ONE

Schooner barge, lost February 4, 1926, three lives lost, foundered off Barnegat.

NUMBER TWENTY-TWO

Schooner barge, lost January 17, 1909, five lives lost, foundered off Barnegat.

NUMBER TWENTY-SIX

Schooner barge, lost November 25, 1907, off Barnegat.

NUMBER TWENTY-EIGHT

Schooner barge, lost February 4, 1926, three lives lost, foundered off Barnegat.

O.H. CANADAY
    Brig, lost November 15, 1871, off Manasquan.
ODDA J. BONNER
    Schooner, lost June 21, 1877, off Barnegat.
OLSEN
    Clam boat, lost April 17, 1961, off Manasquan.
OLIVE T. WHITTIER
    Schooner, lost December 27, 1904, cargo of lumber, wrecked off
    Ship Bottom.
OLIVER SCOFIELD
    Schooner, lost December 4, 1900, off Chadwick Beach.
OLSON
    Oil screw vessel, lost April 17, 1961, foundered off Manasquan.
ONEIDA
    Schooner, lost September 6, 1871, off Manasquan Beach.
ORBIT
    Schooner, lost January 9, 1827, off Manasquan.
ORION
    Bark, lost January 1850, off Manasquan.
ORLANDO V. WOOTTEN
    Schooner, lost April 8, 1922, off Barnegat.
ORLEANS
    Barge, lost 1964, off Long Branch.
OSPREY
    Oil screw vessel, lost July 31, 1852, burned off Asbury Park.
OTHERE
    Schooner, lost May 26, 1878, off Harvey Cedars.
P.H. FALKENBERG
    Schooner, lost October 1868, cargo of coal, off Barnegat.
PACIFIC
    Schooner, lost May 6, 1856, four lives lost, off Long Branch.
PALMELIA
    Schooner, lost November 7, 1842, cargo of lumber, off Deal.
PANDORA
    Schooner, lost February 6, 1880, off Chadwick.
PARK CITY
    Steamer, lost August 7, 1951, off Manasquan.
PEARCE
    Barge, lost September 30, 1944, foundered off Barnegat.
PERKASIE
    Schooner, lost July 8, 1909, off Barnegat.

PETROL
 Schooner, lost October 29, 1879, off Mantoloking.
PHANTON
 Schooner, lost 1856, off Shark River.
PIONEER
 Steamer, lost February 15, 1846, in old Cranberry Inlet.
PLYMOUTH
 Barge, lost March 31, 1924, off Long Branch.
POCOPSON
 Barge, lost October 17, 1936, foundered off Shark River.
POLMQUA
 Sloop, lost October 13, 1834, off Manasquan Beach.
PORGIE
 Sloop, lost September 8, 1769, off Barnegat.
POST BOY
 Schooner, lost April 24, 1828, off Island Beach.
POTMAC
 Schooner, lost January 3, 1840, off Island Beach.
PRIDE OF ARAGON
 Schooner, lost 1889, off Bay Head.

This diver is prepared to go over the side in search of lobsters and artifacts.

PRIDE OF BARNEGAT BAY
Steamship, lost June 2, 1886, in the Barnegat Bay at Seaside Park.
PURITAN
Schooner, lost January 5, 1865, cargo of hides, off Barnegat.
QUEEN
Steamship, lost 1850, two miles off Bay Head.
QUEEN LOUISE
Schooner, lost February 7, 1914, off Manasquan.
R.A. MAGILL
Schooner, lost April 14, 1893, off Manasquan.
R.C. WALDRON
Schooner, lost July 26, 1869, cargo of wood, off Manasquan.
R. FOWLER
Schooner, lost December 22, 1867, on the Barnegat Shoals.
R.G. PORTER
Schooner, lost 1866, off Point Pleasant.
R.J. CORSON
Schooner, lost September 2, 1875, in the Barnegat Inlet.
R.S. DEAN
Schooner, lost December 7, 1868, off Deal.
RED DRAGON
Sloop, lost September 18, 1903, no survivors, off Harvey Cedars.
REGISTER
Brig, lost 1867, on the Barnegat Shoals.
REINDEER
Brig, lost 1867, off Surf City.
RELIANCE
Schooner, lost December 8, 1886, off Barnegat.
RICHARD T. GREEN
Brigantine, lost November 10, 1894, off Ship Bottom.
RICHMOND
Schooner, lost October 20, 1897, off Spring Lake.
RIO GRANDE
Schooner, lost January 16, 1883, off Spring Lake.
ROB ROY
Barge, lost October 5, 1933, off Barnegat.
RODRIGER
Schooner, lost 1909, off Barnegat.
S.E. BARNS
Schooner, lost March 23, 1878, off Barnegat.

S. ELIZA DUNN
Schooner, lost November 24, 1878, off Barnegat.

ST. CROIX
Schooner, lost April 27, 1872, off Shark River.

SADIE
Schooner, lost February 19, 1879, off Point Pleasant.

SALLY
Sloop, lost September 8, 1769, cargo of 30 barrels of mackerel, six lives lost, wrecked off Barnegat.

SAMUEL CASTERS
Schooner, lost December 7, 1880, off Forked River.

SAMUEL WILLETTS
Ship, lost July 1, 1857, off Manasquan.

SAN JUAN
Spanish brig, lost March 4, 1866, off Barnegat.

SAN LUIS
Steamship, lost March 21, 1852, off Manasquan.

SARA H. BLAISDELL
Schooner, lost August 12, 1928, off Seaside Park.

SARAH QUINN
Schooner, lost December 23, 1878, off Mantoloking.

SCIOTO
Schooner, lost March 18, 1852, off Long Beach Island.

SCUDD
Schooner, lost March 27, 1870, cargo of corn and flour, off Manasquan.

SEA KING
Oilscrew vessel, lost March 1963, in the Barnegat Inlet.

SEARSPORT
Barge, lost February 4, 1926, four lives lost, off Barnegat.

SENATE
Schooner, lost January 8, 1840, off Manasquan Beach.

SETH H. LINTHICUM
Barge, lost July 19, 1935, off Barnegat.

SEVERENCE R. ROPER
Schooner, lost August 18, 1884. Collided with the S.S. Kate Fawcett off Barnegat.

SHOOTING STAR
Schooner, lost March 16, 1865, off Barnegat.

SIMALA
Schooner, lost January 6, 1877, off Harvey Cedars.
SOLON
Schooner, lost February 5, 1827, off Island Beach.
SOUTH
Brig, lost 1856, off Point Pleasant.
SOUTH CAROLINA
Steamer, lost December 22, 1874, cargo of rice, raisins, cotton and dry goods, wrecked in the Barnegat Inlet.
SOUTHERNER
Schooner, lost November 7, 1873, cargo of ice, two lives lost, wrecked off Shark River.
SOVERIGN
Ship, lost February 16, 1835, off Manasquan.
SPEED
Schooner, lost 1859, off Manasquan.
SPLENDID
Schooner, lost February 3, 1831, off Long Branch.

The Shorthorn Sculpin is a rare visitor to the inshore wrecks. Photo by Herb Segars.

The German submarine U833 was one of many that roamed our waters during World War II. Photo by Joe Milligan.

SPRITE
    Schooner, lost March 30, 1881, off Barnegat.
STARLIGHT
    Steamship, lost October 5, 1866, stranded off Barnegat.
STELLA
    Bark, lost July 25, 1869, cargo of corn, off Deal.
STEPHEN D. BARNES
    Steamship, lost December 25, 1875, off Barnegat.
STEPHEN J. FOOKS
    Schooner, lost February 1889, off Barnegat.
SUB CHASER #60
    U.S. Naval vessel, lost October 1, 1918, 1.5 miles off Shrewsbury
    in 75 feet of water.
SUCCESS
    Sloop, lost December 8, 1763, off Manasquan.
SUCCESS
    Sloop, lost March 1779, off Island Beach.
SULTANA
    Schooner, lost 1864, off Long Beach.

The Varanger's bell shortly after it was recovered in 1983. Photo by Joe Milligan.

SURPRISE
   Schooner, lost April 4, 1815, off Island Beach.
SUSAN H. RITCHIE
   Schooner, lost April 11, 1894, off Bay Head.
SUSAN SNOW
   Oilscrew vessel, lost March 6, 1966, off Manasquan.
SYLAN GLEN
   Schooner, lost July 3, 1886, off Barnegat.
SWAN
   Brigantine, lost March 8, 1731, off Manasquan.
TAROLINTA
   Schooner, lost July 23, 1886, burned off Barnegat.
TARTAR
   Ship, lost February 2, 1867, off Deal Beach.
TARTAR
   Gas screw vessel, lost August 1, 1915, off Barnegat.
TASSO
   Schooner, lost December 10, 1856, off Barnegat.
THE QUEEN
   British steamship, lost February 25, 1875, off Manasquan.
THOMAS FLETCHER
   Bark, lost February 4, 1875, off Manasquan.
THOMAS G. SMITH
   Schooner, lost February 10, 1878, off Shark River.
THANKFUL WINSLOW
   Schooner, lost February 3, 1830, off Manasquan.
THREE FRIENDS
   Schooner, lost December 3, 1810, off Manasquan Beach.
TRANSIT
   Schooner, lost April 14, 1881, in the Barnegat Bay.
TREMLET
   Schooner, lost 1856, off the Barnegat Shoals.
TRURO
   Barge, lost May 26, 1934, 2 lives lost, off Barnegat.
TSENGORA
   Ship, lost March 29, 1886, cargo of empty kerosene barrels, off
   Spring Lake.
TUNKHANNECK
   Schooner, lost October 18, 1914, off Barnegat.
TWO FRIENDS
   Sloop, lost January 1778, cargo of salt, molasses, rum and sugar.
   One life lost, wrecked off Barnegat.

UDOLA
  Ship, lost February 14, 1871, cargo of dried fruit, off Barnegat.
UNDERWRITER
  Schooner, lost April 1851, off Manasquan.
VANDAL
  Schooner, lost April 22, 1897, off Seaside Heights.
VEGA
  Oilscrew vessel, lost January 11, 1961, off Shark River.
VELEZ
  Schooner, lost February 12, 1881, off Point Pleasant.
VICTORIA
  Italian bark, lost December 24, 1871, cargo of salt, came ashore
  off Shark River.
VICTORY
  Schooner, lost January 19, 1928, off Barnegat Light.
VILLOTINE
  Italian bark, lost December 26, 1871, cargo of marble, foundered
  off Manasquan.
VINDAL
  Norwegian steamship, lost April 22, 1918, cargo of hides and
  coffee, wrecked on the Barnegat Shoals.

Big humpback seabass can often fill the cooler quickly. Photo by Captain Paul Regula.

Exploring the unknown has always fascinated many divers. Photo by Herb Segars.

W.C. WARNER
    Brig, lost October 30, 1886, cargo of sugar, off Mantoloking.
WALKER
    Schooner, lost 1860, off Barnegat.
WALTER IRVING
    Schooner, lost March 7, 1872, cargo of corn, off Barnegat.
WASHTENAW
    Steamship, lost May 8, 1908, cargo of petroleum, off Chadwick.
WEST JERSEY
    Ferry boat, lost November 23, 1885, in the Barnegat Bay.
WILLIAM & ANNE
    Brig, lost July 1, 1777, off Deal.
WILLIAM COLLYER
    Schooner, lost October 23, 1878, off Harvey Cedars.
WILLIAM D. BECKER
    Schooner, lost April 7, 1907, foundered off Barnegat.
WILLIAM HUPER
    Schooner, lost July 1884, off Barnegat.
WILLIAM MOWRAY
    Schooner, lost November 7, 1842, off Deal.

WILLIAM THOMPSON
Schooner, lost October 10, 1879, off Barnegat.
WILMORE
Schooner, lost November 24, 1901, off Chadwick Beach.
WILSON AND HUNTING
Schooner, lost November 9, 1904. Collided with the vessel Culgoa off Barnegat.
WILSON C. HUNTING
Schooner, lost November 9, 1904, off Barnegat.
XEBEC
Schooner, lost April 14, 1880, off Barnegat.
YALE
Schooner, lost December 26, 1890, wrecked off Deal.
YANKEE
Freighter, lost June 11, 1919. Wreck rests in 110 feet of water off Long Branch.
YUMCHI
Brig, lost 1848, cargo of tea and silk, off Long Beach Island.
ZAMPA
Lost off Manasquan Inlet.
ZETLAND
Brig, lost November 2, 1881, off Manasquan.

SOME SELECTED REFERENCES

Berg, Daniel. Shore Diver. New York: Aqua Explorers, Inc. 1987.

Berg, Daniel. Wreck Valley. New York: Aqua Explorers, Inc. 1986.

Berg, Daniel. Wreck Valley II. New York: Aqua Explorers, Inc. 1990.

Berg, Daniel and Denise. Tropical Shipwrecks. New York: Aqua Explorers, Inc. 1989.

Berman, Bruce. Encyclopedia of American Shipwrecks. Massachusetts: Mariners Press 1972.

Davis, Bill. Shipwrecks Off The Central New Jersey Coast. New Jersey: Privately Published 1987.

Downey, Leland Woolley. Broken Spars. New Jersey: Brick Township Historical Society 1983.

Farb, Roderick. Shipwrecks. Alabama: Menasha Ridge Press 1985.

Figley, Bill. A Guide To Fishing and Diving New Jersey's Artificial Reefs. New Jersey: Bureau of Fish and Wildlife 1989.

Gentile, Gary. Advanced Wreck Diving Guide. Maryland: Cornell Maritime Press 1988.

Gentile, Gary. Andrea Doria: Dive To An Era. Pennsylvania: Gary Gentile Productions 1989.

Gentile, Gary. USS San Diego. Pennsylvania: Gary Gentile Productions 1989.

Gentile, Gary. Shipwrecks of New Jersey. Connecticut: Sea Sport Publications 1988.

Siebold, David and C. Adams. Shipwrecks and Legends Around Cape May. New Jersey: Privately Published 1987.

Siebold, David and C. Adams. Shipwreck, Sea Stories and Legends of The Delaware Coast. Pennsylvania: Exeter House Books 1989.

Siebold, David and C. Adams. Legends of Long Beach Island. New Jersey: Privately Published 1985.

Siebold, David and C. Adams. Shipwrecks Near Barnegat. New Jersey: Privately Published 1984.

Siebold, David and C. Adams. Shipwrecks off Ocean City. New Jersey: Privately Published 1986.

Waypoint Notes

_____

_____

_____

_____

_____

_____

_____

_____

_____

_____

_____

_____

_____

_____

_____

_____

_____

_____

ABOUT THE AUTHOR

Born and raised in Bristol, Pennsylvania, Bill Davis spent many summers at the Jersey shore where he became interested in fishing and boating. He later moved to Toms River, New Jersey and soon became involved in diving. Initially certified in 1979, Bill has been diving for over eleven years. In addition to his basic open water certification he also earned night diver, research diver, deep diver, wreck diver, dive master and assistant instructor certifications.

Preferring wreck diving to other forms, Bill has logged over 700 dives, many on wrecks off the New Jersey coastline. In preparing for these dives he has collected a great deal of information pertaining to the wrecks and has built an extensive file that includes over 1,000 shipwrecks. A brief history of the vessel is included in each file along with location coordinates and photographs for many of these wrecks.

His many dives have included various locations along the eastern seaboard. Included in this dive log are the Mercedes wreck off Fort Lauderdale, the German submarines U-85 and U-352 off North Carolina and the Andrea Doria off Montauk, Long Island.

He enjoys collecting wreck artifacts. Drawing on his knowledge of a wreck, Bill finds a suitable location and begins fanning the sand. Among the many pieces in his collection are numerous portholes, ammunition rounds off the USS San Diego, flatware from the U-85, china from the Andrea Doria, silverware from the Oregon and the ship's bell from the wooden steamship Delaware.